Grow Your Own Vegetables

Practical Advice on Growing the Organic Way

Grow Your Own Vegetables

Practical Advice on Growing the Organic Way

KEVIN FORBES

Abbeydale Press

Published by Abbeydale Press
an imprint of Bookmart Ltd
Registered number 2372865
Trading as Bookmart Ltd
Blaby Road, Wigston, Leicester
LE18 4SE, England

Produced by Omnipress Limited, UK
Cover design by Omnipress Limited, UK

THE AUTHOR

KEVIN FORBES lives in East Sussex and is an RHS
qualified gardener. He has a wide knowledge of
horticulture and likes to share this with his reader. He
says he puts his love of gardening down to his mother,
whose enthusiasm rubbed off on him. He is currently
running his own gardening and property
maintenance company.

PUBLISHER'S NOTE

Although the advice and information in this book
are believed to be accurate and true at the time
of going to press, neither the authors nor the
publisher can accept any legal responsibility or
liability for any errors or omissions that may be
made nor for any inaccuracies nor for any harm or
injury that comes about from following instructions
or advice in this book.

CONTENTS

INTRODUCTION

WHY GARDEN ORGANICALLY?

The lack of harmful chemicals on the foods your family consumes and in the ecosystem that is your garden, is reason enough to practise organic gardening. There is no harm done to the environment, and you will feel as if you are doing your part to protect our planet. Learning the proper techniques needed to avoid disease and grow healthy plants is an important part of organic gardening.

It is not only chemicals on fruit and vegetables that can harm you and you family, the mere presence of these chemicals in our garden sheds increases the chances of an accidental poisoning. Even when used according to instructions, many weed killers and pesticides can cause skin and eye irritation. Water that leaches chemicals used on your land will eventually reach a natural waterway posing a hazard to aquatic life, and the ecosystem in general.

The best substance you can apply to your garden doesn't come from a garden or DIY centre; it comes from your compost bin. You have the power to significantly improve your garden's soil with leaves, grass clippings and food scraps that would otherwise go into the landfill.

In more ways than one, organic gardening doesn't cost the earth! The aim of organic growing is to grow healthy plants, and you achieve this by creating healthy growing conditions by providing an environment where there is a good balance of wildlife and organisms that keeps pests in check. Banishing harmful chemicals from the garden not only stops you eradicating beneficial insects and animals; it also saves you money. The materials required for organic gardening are cheap, if not free:

- Free garden compost is the most important way of creating ideal growing conditions.
- Well rotted manure is cheaper than non-organic fertilizer and is far better for the garden.
- Encourage beneficial insects by growing plants that are attractive to them.
- A pond will attract frogs and toads, and these will keep slugs in check.
- Keep larger pests like rabbits out of the garden by using wire netting on fences and repellent scents.
- Mulches not only keep moisture in the ground, but also encourage spiders and beetles that feed on pests.
- Physical barriers like stem collars can be made from recycled materials.

In the organic garden the plants and crops will not always be perfect. Sometimes the pests will have the upperhand, and plants will die and crops fail, but always see it as work in progress. You now have a space for another plant, and knowledge to choose something that may be more suitable for the current conditions. The non-organic gardener can similarly experience less than healthy plants and crops, and he also has a garden poisoned with chemicals. The non-organic gardener will probably not learn from problems, but continue to grow the same plants in the same conditions and think that maybe the cure is another type of chemical.

THE ORIGINS OF ORGANIC GROWING

Of course, there was once a time when the growing of all crops and other plants was done organically. There were no artificial chemicals available, and man had to grow in harmony with nature. This meant he had a great depth of knowledge of ecosystems, and how to make them work to his advantage.

Non-organic fertilizers and pesticides were first introduced in the 19th century, but it was just after the Second World War that using man-made chemicals on soil and plants — both farm and garden — became almost routine. Indeed, two chemicals that had been used in quantity for warfare were adapted for peace-time agricultural purposes. Ammonium nitrate, a key component of many explosives, became an abundant and cheap source of nitrogen-rich fertilizer, and DDT, which had been developed to control disease-carrying insects around troops, became a general insecticide.

Who is responsible for the original promotion of organic growing methods? There are a number of people who can be credited with this, among them:

- In Germany in the 1920s, Rudolf Steiner's development, biodynamic agriculture, included within it many of the essential aspects of what we now call organic farming.

- From 1905 to 1924, the British botanist Sir Albert Howard worked as an agricultural adviser in Bengal, India, where he documented traditional Indian farming practices, and came to regard them as superior to conventional agricultural science. He published his thoughts in 1940 in his book *An Agricultural Testament*.

- Also in 1940, Lord Northbourne was the first to use the term 'organic farming' in his book *Look to the Land*. The term derives from his concept of 'the farm as organism'.

- In 1939, strongly influenced by Sir Howard's work, Lady Eve Balfour launched the Haughley Experiment on farmland in England: a comparison of organic and conventional farming. Four years later she published *The Living Soil,* based on her research. This lead to the formation of a key international organic group: the Soil Association.

• During the 1950s, American playwright, editor, author and publisher J.I. Rodale began to popularise the term and methods of organic growing. In addition to agricultural research, Rodale's publications through the Rodale Press helped to promote organic gardening to the general public.

• In 1962, Rachel Carson, a prominent scientist and naturalist, published *Silent Spring,* chronicling the effects of DDT and other pesticides on the environment. A bestseller in many countries, *Silent Spring* was instrumental in the US government's 1972 banning of DDT. The book and its author are often credited with launching the environmental movement.

WHAT IS ORGANIC GARDENING?

To be certified organic, agricultural products must be grown and manufactured in a manner that adheres to standards set by the country they are sold in. In the United Kingdom these standards are set by the Organic Farmers and Growers Association, and the Soil Association.

Defining the term 'organic gardening' is not quite so clear cut. Organic gardening is not regulated and people can set their own standards: quite common to find someone who regards themselves as organic, but is happy to use slug pellets or systemic weedkiller. Organic gardening is sometimes defined as gardening without the use of chemicals, but this is an awkward and negative definition. Negative definitions are cumbersome because the gardener needs to know what he can or should use, and why. Also, it is not possible to avoid the use of 'chemicals' in gardening because every gas, liquid and solid are 'chemical' and have a chemical composition. Sulphur, for example, is a basic chemical element. It is also a material that is found in nature. It is mined from natural deposits; it is an essential plant nutrient; it has also been used for well over a hundred years as an insecticide and fungicide. Sulphur is relatively low in toxicity and relatively friendly to the environment. It is included in virtually every list of acceptable materials for use on Certified Organic Crops.

Organic gardening is sometimes defined along the lines of 'that kind of gardening that only employs materials from natural sources.' A problem with this definition is that it does not include cultural practices such as the use of disease or pest resistant plants and crop rotation, etc. Cultural practices are vital and should be considered as core issues in organic gardening.

A true definition acknowledges the various aspects and facets of organic gardening: organic gardening is growing plants using only environmentally friendly products, and employing environmentally friendly cultural practices.

THE SOIL

TYPES OF SOIL

Soil is the heart of the organic garden; soil provides vital nutrients and a healthy environment that nurtures plants as they grow. Knowing the soil you are gardening on will help you provide the healthiest growing conditions for your plants. Healthy plants are stronger and better able to withstand pests and disease.

When we talk about soil types, we generally mean the composition, for example, the proportions of clays, sands, silt, minerals and humus (decayed and decaying organic matter) present in the soil. This composition of soil is important because it affects the nutrient content and the texture of the soil, and therefore its aeration and water retention properties. Here is a brief description of the soils you may encounter. Of course these are only the basic types, the soil in any location may be a combination of one or more of them: for example, there are clay loams and sandy loams.

CLAY

A clay soil will feel heavy and sticky when wet, and will hold together when rolled into a thin cylinder.

Clay is very fine-grained, and smooth and silky to the touch. Even when it is well drained it is wet, and so is difficult to cultivate during rainy periods and in the winter months. In fact, if it is worked on when wet, it can be damaged as you may form a compacted layer under your cultivated layer. This 'panning,' as it is known, can be almost impermeable to water so will not easily drain away.

Clays should be dug in the autumn; the soil is then left rough so that the action of the frost and wind can pulverise it and thus improve the structure.

It is most important to see that clay soils are drained, and this is one of the best ways of improving them. They should be cultivated to as great a depth as possible (without mixing subsoil and topsoil), and incorporating manure and compost will improve its structure by encouraging the formation of crumbs. Lime should be applied to clay soils regularly and a really sticky clay soil can be put right quite dramatically with a dressing of lime as it prevents them from becoming so 'sticky', and 'opens' them up. The lime coaxes the individual clay particles to form crumbs and this allows moisture to drain, and gives plant roots the freedom to roam.

The positive aspect of clay soils is that they are much richer in plant nutrients than sand, and also their water-retention properties make them valuable in a dry season.

SANDY SOIL

A sandy soil feels gritty to the touch, and will not hold together or be formed into a ball even when moist.

Sandy soil is relatively infertile because the open nature of the soil means that nutrients are washed away (leached) with the free draining water. As well as irrigation they need frequent feeding. Well rotted manure and compost will improve the soil's structure and water retention, as well as providing nutrients. A sandy soil can also be improved by adding small amounts of clay (marling).

Sandy soil warms up much more quickly in the spring due to its dryness; for this reason it is useful in producing early crops. Another of the advantages of a sandy soil is that it can be worked at any time of the year, and it is comparatively easy to cultivate.

SILTY SOILS

Silty soils are considered to be among the most fertile of soils. They have a slightly soapy, slippery texture, and do not clump easily. Silt is often found on low-lying land near river estauries because the fine particles are washed downstream and deposited when the water flows more slowly. It holds a lot of water, but the slightly larger particles make it a little better at draining than clay. As with clay soils, drainage can be improved by the addition of organic matter.

LOAM

A loam soil is an ideal soil as it has all the advantages of sandy and clay soils, and none of their disadvantages. The sand keeps the soil open, and the clay, in its turn, ensures that sufficient moisture and nutrient retention properties are there.

Loam is generally considered the best soil for growing most types of plants. A loam will not need work to improve its stucture, but will still benefit from the addition of manure and compost for nutrients and to encourage soil organisms.

CHALKY SOIL

Chalky soils are usually rather shallow and stoney with fine particles of chalk or limestone. They are often very lacking in nutrients, and as much organic matter as possible should be added every year.

Because of the chalk present, the leaves of plants often become bright yellow in colour, owing to what is known as chlorosis. This yellowing may not affect the plants in any other way, but it usually means stunted growth.

Probably the only advantage to a chalky soil is that it is seldom necessary to lime it, and the clubroot disease which affects brassicas is not usually a problem.

PEAT SOIL

Peat soil is dark, rich in organic matter and moisture rententive. Peat is formed when damp, acidic conditions prevent full decomposition of organic matter. Peaty soil is rich in humus and does not usually benefit from the addition of compost or manure; it is usually very 'sour' and often completely devoid of lime. Peat is often found in low-lying areas, and so may be waterlogged and therefore need pipe-draining.

Certain crops, like celery and acid loving plants, such as rhododendrons and azaleas, do very well on peat soils. Once peat soils are well worked and limed they can be very healthy and productive.

SOIL ACIDITY AND ALKALINITY (pH)

The term pH refers to the acidity or alkalinity of your soil. Soil pH can be tested with simple test kits available at most garden centres. Follow the instructions carefully, and take a number of samples as they can vary over even a small area. The most acidic substances have a pH rating of 1; with the most alkaline substances a rating of 14; a neutral soil type has a pH rating of 7. Most soils, however, fall within the range of 5 to 9.

It is important to know the pH of your soil because extremes below pH5.5 (acid) and above pH7.5 (alkaline) can be problematic, with increases in certain pests, diseases and nutritional disorders. Magnesium deficiency and clubroot are more prevalent on acid soils, while trace element deficiencies are common on particularly alkaline soils.

ACIDIFYING SOIL

Trying to acidify soil can be difficult and expensive. The most popular material for this purpose has been peat; however, due to the effects its extraction has on wildlife habitats and the enviroment, this is not desirable. Adding manure will lower the pH of your soil. If you wish to grow plants like blueberries, rhododendrons and azaleas, and you have alkaline soil, it is best to grow them in containers of ericaceous John Innes compost.

Another option worth trying if your soil is fairly neutral, are coffee grounds (coffee bars will often give them to you free). These will acidify the soil when added to planting holes and used as mulch.

LIMING

If you have a neutral or acidic soil then it is certainly worth liming the soil every few years, especially on vegetable plots and grassed areas. There are several types of lime: slaked lime is the most commonly available, often simply called 'garden lime'. This lasts about two years. Ground limestone (sometimes called dolomite lime) is slightly better than slaked lime as it lasts longer in the soil (three years or more) and also contains magnesium. Calcified seaweed is the most expensive way of liming your soil, but this also contains many trace elements. Hydrated lime, often called 'builders lime', is cheap, but lasts for a year at most.

The amount required will depend upon the soil type and the degree of pH increase desired. Lime should not be added at the same time as organic material as they will counter react. Liming should be done at least one month before planting anything in the soil.

If both manure or compost and lime are required add the organic material first (around October), and lime in February/March. If just liming is required it should be applied to clay soil in autumn, or to sandy soil in spring.

Lime can be spread on the surface of the soil or grass and left for rain to wash it in. On vegetable plots with medium to heavy soils it is better to dig it in to the top spit of soil.

Lime will not be required each year, and in a vegetable crop rotation every three or four years should be adequate. Liming should be done before planting brassicas or peas but not before potatoes.

WATER

The water available in the soil is crucial to a plant's health. Providing the correct amount of water is one of the most important ways of ensuring good growing conditions. Outdoors in open ground, rainfall will keep most plants growing in beds and borders happy for much of the time. Only in hot, dry summers is supplementary watering needed. Plants growing in pots, hanging baskets, tubs, window boxes and other containers will need watering regularly.

In times of drought it is better to give plants a drench once or twice a week rather than a little water every day. The water needs to soak down to the roots and just a small amount will not penetrate the surface as it will evaporate in the heat.

Make the most of winter and spring rains and conserve the moisture in the soil by using mulches. Always apply the mulch when the ground is already moist, otherwise it may only prevent rain getting to the roots, where it is needed.

Water in the evening to avoid the effects of transpiration and evaporation.

One way to help the water reach the roots is to use plastic bottles: cut the bottoms and stick them upside down like funnels into the soil next to plants. Pour a litre or so into these bottles and let the water drain into the soil. This is not only an efficient way of preventing water loss, but it also speeds up the watering process.

Rain water is often better for plants than tap water, especially for acid lovers; most tap water is fairly alkaline. Conserve rain water by having as many water butts as possible; catch the run-off from all available gutters and roofs. The temperature of water in rain barrels will be nearer to that of the soil, and so less of a shock to tender plants than water from the tap. Irrigate plants in the greenhouse with water that has been allowed to warm up a little. Once you have watered, fill the watering cans and leave them in the greenhouse until the next watering is due, and then use the warmed water.

When planting a new shrub in hot and dry conditions, prune and reduce the leafy growth in order to lessen the water loss while the plant is establishing itself. Bedding plants benefit from having all buds removed as you are planting them, especially if they are a little leggy. This will give the roots time to settle down before expending too much energy in producing flowers.

Vegetables need watering at certain times of their growing cycle. For example, water potatoes when the tubers begin to form; soft fruit, as the fruit sets; leafy vegetables, as the hearts begin to develop; peas and beans, when they are flowering.

Make the best of drought resistant plants like Cytisus, Euphorbia, Helianthemum, Lavendula, Nepeta, Rosemary, Senecio, Sage and Thyme, and conserve water for the plants that need it.

Improve the absorbency of the soil by adding humus in the form of garden compost and well rotted manure.

NUTRIENTS

Plants need certain minerals to exist. These nutrients are absorbed from the soil through the roots; they then mix with water and carbon dioxide to make food.

Macronutrients such as nitrogen, potassium and phosphorus are required in large amounts. Nitrogen encourages leafy growth; potassium is needed for healthy fruits and flowers, and phosphorus is for root growth. Other macronutrients are calcium, magnesium and sulphur. Plants also need micronutrients — or trace minerals — including iron, boron, copper, manganese, molybdenum, zinc, and chlorine.

BENEFITS OF ORGANIC OVER INORGANIC FERTILISER

Soluble inorganic fertilisers contain high percentages of nutrient (nitrogen, phosphorus and potassium) in consistent and reliable proportions. These nutrients are present naturally in the soil, and as they are used by the plants they need to be replaced and replenished. It is not natural, however, to have these nutrients in the very high concentrations that occur when inorganic fertilisers are used. It is rather like feeding children junk food because they are quick-acting and so rich. They are especially unsuitable for sandy soils because most of the nutrient may be leached away.

Slow release inorganic fertilisers have been developed to overcome some of the drawbacks of soluble inorganic fertiliser. They are, however, expensive and, since they rely on soil temperature and moisture content to break down the formulations, they are not always reliable and predictable. Nature has provided better slow release fertilisers in the form of manure and compost; these can be viewed as being the healthy wholefood alternative to the junk food artificial fertiliser.

Weight for weight, well-rotted manure and garden compost contains far lower levels of the main macronutrients than inorganic fertiliser. However, this is not comparing like for like. Unlike inorganic fertilisers, manures and composts contain high levels of micronutrients and all of the nutrients are released over a long term. This long term release of nutients is partly brought about because of the way the bulky nature of these soil additives improves the soil's structure and retentiveness, and partly because some of the nutrients present have to be processed by the soil's micro-organisms before they can be available to the plants.

COMPOST

Garden compost is used to condition and feed the soil. With the exception of peaty soil, the addition of compost will improve any soil. Clay soil becomes crumbly and retains the correct amount of water without water-logging, and sandy soil will retain moisture and therefore also nutrients.

A compost bin or heap is an essential component for any organic garden. It provides a green solution to disposing of vegetable matter, and recycles it back into the garden, reducing the need for externally produced compost. Composting your kitchen and garden waste is also the single most effective thing you can do to reduce the amount of rubbish you send to the land fill. Up to 30% of what goes into an average dustbin can be composted down to make a useful soil improver.

The simplest bin can be made from wire netting about 1 m (3 ft) high, strung around four stakes hammered into the ground. The problem with this simple bin is that it gives you no control over temperature or moisture content, and you need this control to make the best compost in the quickest time.

Garden waste will only turn to compost if there is sufficient heat. Within limits, the higher the temperature of the compost heap, the quicker it will become usable. The peak temperature of a compost heap is 60°C (140°F); at this temperature, it will compost quickly and destroy any rogue weed seeds that found their way into the heap.

Achieve the best possible temperature by positioning in a warm site and by making it a decent size — the larger the compost heap the higher its temperature. One metre (3 ft) square, by 1 m (3 ft) high is ideal.

It is very easy to make a moveable wooden compost bin consisting of identical interlocking sections stacked on top of each other. Make these box sections using 4 wooden boards, approximately 1 m (3 ft) long and 7.5 cm (3 in) wide, and 2.5 cm (1 in) thick. Attach together with four 5 cm (2 in) x 5 cm (2 in) wooden pegs at each corner, 7.5 cm (3 in) long. The pegs should protrude on one side by 2.5 cm (1 in) and this is how the sections interlock. You will need a lid to keep the heat in and stop nutrients from being washed away; this can be made from wood, or an old rug or carpet made from natural materials.

Because this compost bin can have sections added to it as organic matter is added, or sections taken away as the pile rots and decreases in volume; the top sections of the box can be used to start building up a new container. Make a few extra sections and you will have a very flexible composting system.

Of course, you can also buy very good ready made compost bins from garden and DIY centres. Local authorities sometimes sell compost bins at a subsidised rate because the more waste that is composted means that less waste is processed by the environment departments.

After building or acquiring your compost bin you must now choose a site. A compost bin is not an object of beauty even to the most ardent organic grower, so the bin needs to be out of sight; but, in hiding the bin, do not put it in a shady place as it needs as much heat from the sun as is possible. For the same reason, if possible, provide shelter from wind that may cool it down. Try to place a compost bin or heap directly on the soil so it can absorb all the micro-organisms.

The soil for 1 m (3 ft) around your compost heap will be rich in nutrients; this would be an ideal spot for something like rhubarb, sunflowers or hollyhocks but do not position the compost heap too near trees or shrubs; the roots of these plants may surface and grow into the compost heap. If you have a full compost heap in early summer that will not be used until the autumn, you can soften its look by growing nasturtiums on it. The plant roots will go deep into the compost and make it more 'crumbly' by aerating it. When the plants die in the autumn just dig them into the heap, and they will return all the goodness they have extracted. You can also plant crops like courgettes or cucumbers on the heap.

The key to making a good compost quickly is to add organic material of different densities in layers of approximately 5 cm (2 in) deep. For one layer use a mixture of fine materials such as (grass clippings, tea leaves, coffee grounds, small weeds), for another use intermediate materials (shredded paper, kitchen waste) and for other layers use coarser materials such as (shrub clippings, straw and large weeds). The sequence of the layers is not important, but the layering process means that too much of one type of material is not kept together. When you have these layers the heat from the grass clippings will boost the decomposition of the shrub clippings. The air circulating around the coarser materials and moisture from the finer materials are required by the micro-organisms that process the contents of the heap.

Grass cutttings and other fine materials can provide a good amount of feed for the micro-organisms in the heap; although the addition of bone meal, animal manure, or similar will speed the composting process considerably. These materials are known as compost activators.

Examples of material suitable for composting:

- Uncooked vegetable peelings and fruit
- Rabbit and guinea pig bedding
- Torn, shredded or scrunched up paper and cardboard (e.g. egg boxes/toilet roll tubes)
- Coffee grounds, tea bags and leaves
- Grass cuttings
- Young or annual weeds not in seed
- Houseplants and flowers
- Finely chopped or shredded shrub prunings
- Wood ash

• Eggshells

Do not compost:

• Cooked food, fish, meat scraps and bones (may all encourage rats)
• Pernicious weeds (such as bindweed, thistle, dock roots and ground elder) or any weeds that have gone to seed
• Magazines
• Coal ash and soot
• Large woody branches
• Cat litter or dog faeces

Because you never have the same quantity of composting materials available at the same time, keep your coarser materials in a bin or heap to one side of your composting bin. These shrubby clippings can be chopped up with a sharp spade or secateurs when convenient, and then added to the compost pile after a layer of finer materials.

Regularly turn the contents of the compost bin (once a month). This involves taking a fork to the heap and mixing up the contents. This is because the compost will sag as it decomposes and the air pockets that you have created in the layering process will cease to exist. Turning the partly processed compost will re-introduce air and speed up the activity of the micro-organisms. The other benefit of regular turning of the heap is that it will discourage rats from visiting.

Normally, materials like grass clippings and kitchen waste provide enough moisture to the micro-organisms, but if a lot of coarser materials are used it may be necessary to apply a small amount of water from time to time. Straw, in particular, can cause a compost heap to become too dry, so water the straw before adding it to the heap. Don't let the heap become too wet though as this is worse than too little water.

Given the best conditions you should have good compost about three months after the heap has been started. The finished material will be crumbly and brown, moist but not wet and have a slightly sweet smell.

The quality may vary within the heap, with some parts only half decomposed. This usually happens when the compost heap is too small. The solution is to use the good compost to dig into your soil and use what remains to start the next heap. Do not dig partially composted material into your soil: the texture of the soil may be improved, but the process of the material rotting further will rob nutrients from the soil.

Dig the compost into the soil because this will improve the soil's texture and provide a long-lasting supply of slow-release nutrients. An alternative is to use the compost as a mulch, but this would not make the the best use of its qualities.

HORSE AND FARMYARD MANURES

With the exception of peat, any soil can be improved by the addition of manure as the physical condition of it will be improved by incorporating bulky, organic materials. Not only do organic manures supply plant nutrients, but they add substances that have the power to act on the insoluble compounds already in the soil, and so reduce these compounds to a form that plants can use.

Heavy, clay soils are improved by manuring as they become lighter and easier to work. Light, sandy soils are 'bulked-up' by using organic manures and this helps them to retain moisture and nutrients.

Farmyard and horse manures consist of animal excrements, both liquid and solid, and of the litter (usually straw) put down for the animals to lie on. Sometimes sawdust is used as litter; manure containing sawdust should be avoided because the wood takes a long time to rot down. The value of these farmyard manures also varies according to how the animals have been fed and looked after, and the way in which the manure has been stored. The best manure is a mature one that has been made and kept under cover.

If manures are left exposed to the actions of the sun, wind and rain for any length of time, as they often are, then a portion of the nutrient content will have leached out.

Horse manure is probably richer in nutrients than cow manure, although horse manure does lose its value if kept in the open more quickly than cow manure. Pig and sheep manures are richer in nitrogen.

Some stables give away manure freely, especially if it is fresh, as that means it does not take up space or time in storing it. If you have a large garden and somewhere to store a small heap (where the smell will not offend anyone) cover the heap over with a plastic sheet while it matures. One bag of fresh horse manure is useful to keep next to your compost bin; use it as an activator just before and/or after a layer of coarser material.

Dig manure into heavy, clay soils in the autumn or winter; use manures that are well rotted but still contain a small amount of straw. Dig light soils in spring using very well rotted manures with the consistency of compost.

OTHER MANURES AND ORGANIC FERTILISERS

SEAWEED was once often used as manure by gardeners living near to the sea. It is nearly as good as farmyard manure — lower in phosphates but richer in potash. Seaweed manure should be applied at the same rate as farmyard manure.

Pollution of the seas around the coast have reduced the collection and use of seaweed as a manure.

SEAWEED MEAL AND EXTRACTS are also available. They are slow-acting, long-lasting plant foods particularly rich in trace elements. They condition the soil and help to build up the humus structure. Apply on the surface and lightly rake in up to 3 months before planting, by which time it will have been broken down by the soil bacteria.

BONE MEAL is a slow-release form of organic phosphate which promotes strong root growth. It is particularly useful when planting new shrubs and trees.

DRIED BLOOD is very rich in nitrogen so it is good for leafy crops like cabbage and lettuce. It should be used only when the plants are growing strongly. You can mix it with water to make a liquid manure or scatter on the soil and water in.

HOOF AND HORN was once a widely used organic fertiliser but is now becoming hard to find. It is a slow-acting source of organic nitrogen suitable as a dressing for most green vegetable crops and lawns where some colour is needed.

SOOT contains nitrogen, and is valuable because it darkens the soil. It contains no phosphates or potash, and is useful in making heavy soils easier to work and more porous.

NETTLE MANURE is an easily made fertizer from young nettles and water. Nettles have deep roots and therefore they bring up trace elements from deeper soil which, while essential to plant health, can be lacking in top soil that is cropped regularly. Nettle manure can be started in the spring when the young nettles begin to appear, and can be continued throughout the growing season.

Make nettle manure using a watertight, open topped container with a lid — metal or plastic will do. Fill the container with young nettles that have been cut or shredded up. An ideal way to collect these nettles is to run a mower (with collecting box) over them; a small amount of grass included will not matter. With the nettles lightly pressed down, add enough water just to cover them. Put the lid on the container to prevent rainwater causing it to overflow. As the nettles break down, the plant fibres will rise to the top, so after a few days place a weight on the 'mush' to hold it under the water. Use a stiff piece of mesh, slightly smaller in diameter than the container, under the weight. Nettle manure takes about three to four weeks to 'mature' — and it does 'mature' to give a fairly earthy smell, so you may want to place the container somewhere out of the way. More nettles and water, if neccessary, can be added to the container throughout the season. Lift out the weight before adding more nettles — if possible, it is best to leave the old plant fibres in the container until the end of the season and then put them on the compost heap.

Nettle manure needs to be diluted before use; the ideal strength is about the colour of tea; this can be around 1 part manure to 10 parts water.

Diluted nettle manure can be used as a foliar feed in a spray bottle, but it needs to be strained before use to remove the small fibres which will inevitably be floating in the solution and could block the spray.

COMFREY is also used to make a liquid manure. The leaves of this deep-rooting, hardy perennial plant are exceptionally rich in potash and also contain useful amounts of nitrogen and phosphate. Although the *Symphytum officinalis*, the common form native to the British Isles, can be used, the Russian comfrey, *Symphytum x uplandicum*, makes a better fertiliser. Use the same method as for nettle manure.

Comfrey leaves are also useful for adding to the compost bin or heap, but do not add too many in one go as they become a bit slimey and may not rot properly. Intersperse the comfrey leaves with some coarser material like shrub clippings.

GREEN MANURES

Green manures are an inexpensive way to improve soil fertility. They improve the soil's structure as well as the nutrient content. Green manures are plants that are grown not as a crop or for ornamental use, but whose purpose is to be dug into the soil to enrich and improve its structure. They can complement the use of compost and animal manures and are usually used in the vegetable garden, fitted in to the crop rotation scheme. They could also be used elsewhere in the garden whenever there is a gap in time between the preparation of a planting area, and the best planting time.

If grown over a wet season green manures will prevent nutrients being washed out of the soil. The roots penetrate the soil and help hold it in place and this prevents soil erosion. They are particularly useful for sandy soils because they enable the soil to hold on to more water, and not drain away so quickly.

Green manures should be grown densely so the ground is well covered. This will crowd out weeds by depriving them of nutrients, space and light.

The sowing of the green manure needs to be timed so that it will be ready to dig into the ground before the next crop is sown, and without leaving a long gap that leaves the ground bare with the possibility of nutrients leaching out of the soil.

It is somtime desirable to undersow a crop with a green manure. Usually the crop is sown and allowed to establish first, and then the green manure sown later amongst it. For example, sweetcorn can be sown and undersown with a green manure once it is growing strongly and has been cleared of weeds. This saves time in preparation of the land and weeding.

Although usually dug into the ground straight away, green manures can be cut and left on the soils surface to act as a mulch.

When digging in, green manure should not be buried too deep but turned in just under the soil's surface. Chopping it up with a spade first makes digging in easier. Young green plants are easier to dig and more beneficial to the soil than older ones. If, for some reason, the green manure is allowed to grow old and too tough to dig in, it may be better to cut and compost it instead.

Legumes such as beans, peas and lupins are often used as green manures, but they are usually dug into the soil before they flower, while still young and leafy and high in nutrients. Legumes are particularly beneficial because they take nitrogen from the air down to the soil. This nitrogen 'fixing' property of legumes will only happen if certain types of bacteria are present in the soil.

When choosing a green manure choose one that will suit the climate and soil that it will be grown in; this will keep it healthy and reduce pests and diseases. Green manures should not be closely related to the following crop; for example, do not plant any legumes before a pea or bean crop.

The most commonly planted green manures suitable for the British climate include:

ALFALFA, *Medicago sativa* can be sown April until July and can be left 1—2 months or up to a few years.

HUNGARIAN GRAZING RYE can be sown August through to November and can be left in over winter. It is suitable for most types of soil.

MUSTARD can be sown July until September and is ready to be dug in 2—8 weeks after sowing. It is best on moist, fertile ground. It can suffer from clubroot, and so should not be sown before or after cabbages or any other brassicas.

PHACELIA, *Phacelia tanacetifolia* can be sown March until September. Summer sowings are left in the ground for 2 months; late sowings are left to overwinter.

The following green manures are nitrogen fixers:

ALSIKE CLOVER, *Trifolium hybridum* can be sown from April until August and is suitable for damp and acid soils. It can be left to grow for a few months or up to 2 years.

BITTER LUPIN, *Lupinus angustifolius* is a nitrogen fixer and should be sown March—June and left in the ground 2—3 months.

ESSEX RED CLOVER, *Trifolium pratense* is sown April—August and can be left 1—2 months or a few years.

FIELD BEANS, *Vicia faba* are leguminous and can be sown in September and November and left to overwinter.

WINTER TARES can be sown July to September and grown through the winter. It is suitable for heavy soil that is not too acidic.

MULCHING

Mulching is a practice which is adaptable to nearly all gardens. Organic mulches add nutrients and humus to the soil as they decompose, improving its tilth and moisture-holding capacity. By covering (or mulching) the surface of your soil, you can reduce weeds by preventing seed germination or by suppressing the growth of new seedlings. Mulches are generally effective against established perennial weeds. The benefits of bulky organic mulches is that they can provide environments for beneficial organisms to thrive.

A mulch can take several forms:

- a living plant ground cover
- loose particles of organic matter spread over the soil
- sheets of artificial or natural materials laid on the soil surface (although it is preferable to use natural materials so that you do not risk putting any toxins into the soil — e.g. from carpet made with artificial fibres, dyes and backings).

In addition to weed control, mulches may also be used to:

- prevent soil erosion
- reduce pest problems
- aid moisture
- prevent loss of nitrates

- reduce the severity of some diseases, such as tomato blight
- reduce fruit and vegetable spoilage
- moderate soil temperatures

CHOOSING WHICH MULCH TO USE

When choosing which type of mulch you wish to use, you will need to consider the availability, cost, appearance, function and durability.

Bark

Commercially-packaged bark mulches are available shredded as chips, nuggets or chunks. They are usually available from nurseries and landscape companies. Bark mulches are attractive, weed free and decompose slowly. (Cedar and cypress are the slowest types to decompose.)

Use bark mulches around trees, shrubs, roses and in perennial beds.

Cocoa-bean hulls

Cocoa-bean hulls are a by-product of chocolate production. They are light, easy to handle and are an attractive brown colour. Added to this they have a very pleasant aroma — especially for chocolate lovers! They can be expensive, but a mulch of just 2.5 to 5 cm (1 to 2 in) should be sufficient. Cocoa-bean mulches are excellent for annuals, perennials and roses, but generally last only for one growing season.

Coconut fibre (Coir)

Coir is a natural fibre derived from the husk of the coconut. Coir fibre, husk and chip are graded into various particle sizes and formulated to suit the growing application. With its high moisture retention, strong porosity and aeration and balanced pH, coir is used worldwide in commercial and home garden applications.

Grass clippings

Allow lawn clippings to dry before applying to the garden. Fresh, green material may settle and form a dense mat, and usually produces an unpleasant smell. If the lawn has been treated with any type of herbicide or chemical, do not use the clippings until the lawn has been mowed at least two or three times. Of course, grass clippings taken from a weed-infested lawn will undoubtedly contain a large amount of weed seed, so be cautious before using this method as a mulch. Grass clippings do not last long and are best used in vegetable gardens or annual flower beds.

Leaves

Leaves should be shredded or composted before being applied as a mulch. Shredded or composted leaves do not mat down as readily as whole leaves, and are less likely to be blown away and decompose more quickly. They are an excellent mulch for vegetable gardens, raspberry plants, annual flower beds and around trees and shrubs.

Although the leaves of some trees — for example oak — are acid in reaction, they can still be used safely in your garden. The small amounts used have little or no effect on the pH of your soil.

Living mulches (or green manure)

These consist of a dense stand of low-growing plants established prior to or after the main crop. Living mulches (or green manure) can be used as a weed suppressant, preventing soil erosion and nitrate leaching.

Newspaper

Shredded newspapers or whole sheets may be used in a vegetable garden. Most newspapers use organic inks these days, so gardeners do not need to worry about lead contamination. When using newspaper sheets, place a layer of 6 to 8 sheets between plant rows. Water the sheets so that they stick together and to the soil surface, and then weigh them down with soil to prevent them being blown away.

Pine needles

Pine needles are light, airy and decompose slowly making them an ideal mulch. They may last for several years and can be easily removed if necessary. Pine needles are acid in reaction and therefore make excellent mulches for acid-loving plants. They can also be safely used in the vegetable garden and elsewhere in home landscaping.

Polypropylene mulch

A black, woven polypropylene mulch is cost-effective as it can last for up to ten years. Although the initial outlay can be expensive, in the long term labour costs are reduced. This fabric, which can be held down with pegs, stones or by tucking the edges into the soil, is invaluable in suppressing weeds and retaining moisture. It is also advantageous in helping smaller hedge plants get established.

Straw

Straw that is free from crop and weed seed makes an excellent mulch for the vegetable garden and strawberry bed. Suitable materials include wheat, oat and soybean straw. Straw may also provide a winter habitat for mice and other rodents, so avoid using it around trees and shrubs.

Wood chips

Wood chips are an excellent mulching material. The material is made by passing tree and shrub trimmings through a mechanical chipper. Wood chips are best used in landscape plantings, such as around trees, shrubs, roses and in perennial beds.

Fresh wood chips, as they rot down, can leach nutrients out of the soil, so you may wish to choose a more environmentally friendly mulch.

NO-DIG GARDENING

Being an avid organic gardener, I saw with interest an article about 'no-dig' gardening some years ago. Immediately I was hooked, as it explained the advantages of this eco-friendly method of growing nutritious vegetables: it is a cheap, no fuss and completely chemical-free way of gardening. This method is often favoured by organic gardeners as some believe that digging is actually harmful to the soil's well-being. It will not be suitable for all gardeners, as you need to avoid walking on the beds to prevent the soil from compacting. If you would like to try it, however, make your bed and let nature do the hard work for you.

There are many benefits and advantages to using a no-dig system:

- Any suitable area can be used to establish a no-dig bed, as there is plenty of sun, access to organic material and clean water.

- It saves time and effort — especially beneficial if you suffer from back problems.

- The organic medium in the no-dig bed retains its structure and fertility well. This is because the organisms in the soil mix together, and because they are not continually being disturbed they do not lose any of their nutrients.

- The no-dig method reduces water use, insect attack and damage. It also keeps weeds to a minimum.

- This method can be done on a small scale so is suitable for any size of garden.

- Finally, it really really works!

THE GARDENER'S BEST FRIEND

The gardener's best friend is the humble little earth worm. If you make a no-dig bed without a solid bottom — for example, recycle an old water tank by cutting out the bottom — then the worms in the soil underneath and nearby will have easy access. They work their way up from the bottom, aerating and enriching the soil as they go.

The advantages of worms:
- They drag small particles of organic matter into the soil.

- They deposit worm casts or vermicast back onto the soil. Vermicast helps to enrich the soil through the addition of micro-elements and plant-friendly bacteria.

- Tunnelling worms aerate the soil which in turn assists with drainage, moisture retention and provides access for developing plant roots.

Useful snippets:

Mixing worm casts with water to form a sort of weak 'tea' solution makes an amazing, eco-friendly and non-toxic natural fertiliser.

Build a 'worm farm' to help you recycle your organic kitchen scraps. This will produce a free, natural liquid fertiliser at the same time.

HOW TO BUILD A NO-DIG GROWING BED

Materials required:
- A framework, which is suitably robust to contain the soil mixture

- Hay or straw

- Old newspapers

- Compost and well-rotted manure

- Organic fertiliser to boost plant growth

- Water to wet down the material as you go

- A couple of hours to prepare and construct your no-dig bed

- Seeds or seedlings to plant

Method

Choose a sheltered sunny spot for your no-dig bed, away from any large tree roots if possible. Make a framework which is strong enough to contain the soil mix and which won't break down in rainy weather. (Recycled rainwater tanks make ideal no-dig grow beds.) Secure your framework with screws, bolts, twine or strong wire — whichever you have to hand.

The hay bale method:

One way of framing a no-dig bed is to use hay bales. Set up your bales in a rectangle, and then loop and tie a supportive ring of strong twine around the bales to prevent them from collapsing.

Knock in some heavy garden stakes around the outside of the frame to provide extra support. Stakes that are tied with twine have the advantage of being an ideal trellis for climbing beans, tomatoes or cucumbers.

Next, lay a layer of gravel, small rocks, twigs, broken bricks or similar coarse material as a base to make sure your bed has good drainage. Make sure this layer is thick enough to smother any ground weeds.

Next, lay several sheets of newspaper or thick cardboard. Wet this down thoroughly. On top of this spread a few handfuls of blood and bone, or similar (slow release) organic fertiliser.

Add the first layer of hay or straw about 20cm
(8 in) thick. Wet this down as well.

The next layer is about 20 cm (8 in) of manure.
Make sure it is well rotted and free of any weeds.
Water in well. On top of the manure add a layer of
compost, humus, or vegetable scraps.

Add another layer of hay or straw and water in
well. To this add garden lime to help stabilise the
pH levels of the soil.

Add another good, thick layer of well-rotted
manure. Top this layer up with a thick layer, about
20 cm (8 in), of humus, compost, potting mix or
good, clean garden soil. This acts as the base
medium to plant your vegetables in.

You will notice that over time the soil mix in your
no-dig bed will start to subside. This is quite
normal and all you need to do is just top it up with
organic material to maintain a sufficient depth.

Boxes, pots, or even old tyres are another way to a
no-dig garden. Remember, though, with no-dig
gardening you will still need to remove all
perennial weeds by hand.

PLANNING

THE IMPORTANCE OF PLANNING

Planning a garden is important to its success, and this is even more relevent in organic gardening because with good planning you can prevent problems occurring. There are many aspects to planning an organic garden, but in essence it means making the most efficient use of the area, time and other resources that are available to you.

PLANNING THE AREAS OF YOUR GARDEN

You need to decide what you require from your garden, and then prioritise and give the most important facets the most suitable positions. When starting out, try not to be over ambitious, as tending a large plot right at the beginning can become quite a chore. A plot that is 3 m (10 ft) long by 3 m (10 ft) wide is large enough to grow some tomato plants, lettuces, cucumbers, radishes, herbs and some flowers.

Once you have chosen your site draw out a plan on paper. This will make sure that you maxmimise productivity by giving each plant room to grow. Measure the dimensions of your plot and draw a scale model on a piece of graph paper — for example, using 2.5 cm (1 in) square to represent 0.3 m (1 ft) area.

As you draw your plan, keep in your head the amount of space each plant will need when it reaches maturity. Remember that crops that are crowded together are far more susceptible to disease.

The layout of your garden will depend on exactly what you want to plant. Some crops, such as lettuces, radishes and spinach, mature quickly and will therefore not be in the ground very long. Of course, it is possible to harvest them several times during the summer, in which case they will occupy space for a longer period of time.

Other plants, such as tomatoes and peppers, will grow over the course of an entire season. Perennial herbs and flowers also stay in the same spot year after year, and require an increasing amount of space each season.

Make sure you keep a record of your garden plan, as you will need to keep this as a reference for rotating crops the following year. Besides depleting the soil of its vital nutrients, leaving plants in the same spot year after year encourages disease and soil-borne insect predators. This is where the importance of crop rotation comes into its own. No annual plant should be planted in the same spot two years in a row; waiting three years before planting a crop in the same spot is even more beneficial to both plant and soil.

When drawing up your plan it is worth considering planting 'green manure' plants to fix the soil.

Another consideration when planning your plot is the type of plant suited to your site. Plants that are adapted to your climate and soil conditions are easier to grow and require less attention or input. If you do decide to try and grow a plant that is not suitable to your conditions, you will need to boost its natural defences in order to keep it healthy and productive.

Once you have planned your garden for the first year, you need to make a plan for the following year as well. Because crop rotation is so important to keep your soil fertile, it is easier to plan where you are going to plant your crops for the following season now. This will help you remember what was planted where, and so saving you any duplications next year.

So now you know where your plot will be and what you are going to put in it, there is nothing to stop you making a start at becoming an organic gardener.

A YEAR IN THE ORGANIC GARDEN

For the organic gardener the change in seasons brings a variety of different jobs. Whether it is the height of summer, with its wonderful choice of fruit, vegetables and colour or the chilly days of autumn, there is always something to do. Bright crisp days are ideal for pruning and tidying up the garden, while the winter months can be a time of planning what you want to grow in the new season. Use the following planner as a guide to the jobs to do in your organic garden.

I need to stress again that it is important to plan for the year ahead: crop rotation is so important to keep your soil healthy. Draw up a plan of where you will plant what in the next season. This will help you remember what was planted where, and save troubles next year.

It is also worth bearing in mind that it is important to never leave your soil bare over the winter. This is because it will lose organic matter through oxidation. Plant a green manure at the end of the harvest and let it die over the winter, or cover the garden with leaves and straw.

MIDWINTER

Pruning
Remove damaged or diseased growths only.

Plant
Chit potato seed on trays in a light place away from frost.

Feed
Spread lime or calcified seaweed on the soil every couple of years.

JOBS TO DO

4 Check any stored fruit and vegetables to make sure they are not going rotten.

4 Utilise the winter months to make bird boxes, insect traps and bottle cloches.

4 Put out plenty of food for the birds and provide them with water.

4 Plan and make changes to your existing beds and make new ones if necessary. Plan what seeds you want to order for the new growing season.

LATE WINTER

Spray
Spray outdoor peaches and almonds using Bordeaux mixture.

Pruning
Remove damaged or diseased growths only.

Plant
Garlic
Onion sets
Shallots
Shrubs
Trees
Soft fruit

Feed
Spread seaweed on bare vegetable plots.

Sow
(Under cover in a warm place):
Indoor tomatoes
Early peas
Broad beans
Cabbages
Cauliflowers
Lettuce
Spinach
Turnips
Carrots

Radishes
Potatoes

(Under cover in pots):
Onions
Spring onions

Grass
Cut the grass with your mower on a high setting in
mild conditions.

JOBS TO DO

4 Check any stored fruit and vegetables to make
   sure they are not going rotten.

4 Top up greenhouse beds with garden compost.

4 Put out cloches, sheet mulches and low tunnels
   to warm the soil.

4 Inspect woody plants, checking stakes, ties
   and labels.

4 Pick off any big buds on blackcurrants.

4 Empty insect traps and retouch sticky bands.

4 Firm in roots of autumn plantings when hard
   frosts have finished.

EARLY SPRING

Spray
Spray everything with a diluted seaweed solution.
Spray outdoor peaches and almonds with a
Bordeaux solution.

Pruning
Prune less hardy and hollow-stemmed shrubs: for
example buddleias.
Remove old canes from autumn-fruiting
raspberries.
Cut back evergreens and conifer hedges.

Plant
Garlic
Onion sets
Shallots
Artichokes
Asparagus
Potatoes
Evergreens
Shrubs
Trees
Grapevines
Soft fruit
Rhubarb

Feed
Spring greens with comfrey liquid or seaweed
solution. Put sieved compost on grassed areas.

Mulch
Spread mulches under and around everything.

Sow
(Under cover in a warm place):
Tomatoes
Cucumbers
Aubergines
Peppers

(Outside in warm soil or under cover):
Peas
Broad beans
Leeks
Beetroot
Kohl rabi
Cabbages
Cauliflowers
Lettuce
Spinach
Turnips
Carrots
Chards
Salsify
Scorzonera
Parsnips
Herbs
Radishes
Spring Onions
Sweet peas

Grass
Cut grass weekly once it starts to grow quickly.

JOBS TO DO

✔ Check any stored fruit and vegetables to make sure they are not going rotten.

✔ Put down sheet mulches on new ground or green manures.

✔ Compost, dig in or invert green manures.

✔ Move, lay and repair turf in non-frosty weather.

✔ Weed regularly.

✔ Retouch sticky bands.

✔ Protect early flowers and budding plants against frosts.

MID-SPRING

Spray
Spray everything with a diluted seaweed mixture.

Pruning
Cut back most early flowering shrubs once the flowers have died.
Remove seed heads from bulbs as they die back.

Plant
Potato sets
Onion seedlings
Perennial herbs
Evergreens

Feed
Top dress all permanent container plants with compost.

Sow
(Under cover in a warm place):
Tomatoes
Ridge cucumbers
Gherkins
Melons
Courgettes
Marrows
Pumpkins
Sweetcorn
Half-hardy flowers

(*Outside and under cover*):
Peas
Broad beans
French beans
Runner beans
Most brassicas
Lettuces and salad plants
Herbs
Spinach
Turnips
Carrots
Swedes
Salsify
Scorzonera
Radishes
Kohl rabi
Fennel
Leeks
Parsnips
Sweet peas

Grass
Cut the grass weekly.

JOBS TO DO

✔ Use up stored fruit and vegetables and clean out stores once empty.

✔ Take cuttings of herbs and less hardy plants. Repot houseplants.

✔ Weed regularly.

✔ Retouch sticky bands.

✔ Inspect regularly for pests and diseases.

✔ Protect tender flowers, fruitlets and plants against late frosts.

LATE SPRING

Spray
Spray everything with a diluted seaweed mixture.

Pruning
Remove crowded and badly-placed shoots on apricot and peach trees. Cut back most flowering shrubs once the flowers have died. Tie in and support growing climbers and tall herbaceous plants.

Plant
Sweetcorn
Ridge cucumbers
Courgettes } (under cover or in open once the
Marrows } last frost is well past)

Feed
Include compost with all transplants. Feed tomatoes and pot plants with comfrey liquid or a seaweed solution.

Mulch
Spread mulches under and around potatoes.

Sow
(Under cover outside):
Tomatoes
Ridge cucumbers
Gherkins
Melons

Courgettes
Marrows
Pumpkins
Sweetcorn
Half-hardy flowers

(*Outside without cover*):
Peas
Broad beans
French beans
Runner beans
Most brassicas
Lettuces and salad plants
Herbs
Spinach
Turnips
Carrots
Swedes
Salsify
Scorzonera
Radishes
Kohl rabi
Fennel
Leeks
Parsnips
Sweet peas
Wallflowers

Grass
Cut the grass weekly.

JOBS TO DO

✔ Weed everything regularly.

✔ Retouch sticky bands.

✔ Inspect regularly for any sign of pests and diseases, especially aphids, cabbage caterpillars and red spider mite.

✔ Protect tender plants against frosts.

✔ Pay special attention to watering autumn and spring plantings.

EARLY SUMMER

Spray

Spray everything with a diluted seaweed mixture.

Pruning

Deadhead and cut back most flowering shrubs once the flowers have died.
Summer prune grapes and redirect new growths.

Plant

Transplant brassica and leek plants.

Feed

Include compost with all transplants. Feed tomatoes and pot plants with comfrey liquid or a seaweed solution.

Mulch

Spread mulches under and around potatoes.

Sow

Lettuces and salad plants
Beetroot
Kohl rabi
Swedes
Turnips
Spinach
Chicory
Endive
Biennial and perennial flowers

Grass
Cut the grass weekly.

JOBS TO DO

✔ Weed everything regularly.

✔ Inspect regularly for any sign of pests and diseases, especially aphids, cabbage caterpillars, gooseberry sawfly and red spider mite.

✔ Protect fruit from birds.

✔ Thin, harvest and use or preserve ripening fruits.

MIDSUMMER

Spray
Spray everything with a diluted seaweed mixture.
Spray maincrop potatoes with Bordeaux mixture if
warm and humid.

Pruning
Prune plums and flowering and fruiting cherries.
Summer prune apples, pears, red and white
currants and grapes. Continue to deadhead. Cut
back evergreens and conifer hedges.

Plant
Potato sets for late crop.

Feed
Include compost with potato sets.

Sow
Lettuces and salad plants
Carrots
Swedes
Turnips
Chinese cabbage
Winter spinach
Kohl rabi
Chards

Grass
Cut the grass as needed.

JOBS TO DO

✔ Weed everything as needed.

✔ Retouch sticky bands.

✔ Inspect regularly for any sign of pests and diseases.

✔ Protect fruit and provide water for birds.

✔ Thin, harvest and use or preserve ripening fruits.

✔ Dry peas and beans for use as seed in kitchen.

✔ Dry and freeze herbs.

✔ Dry onions and garlic in the sun.

✔ Use or store early potatoes to free ground for further sowing.

LATE SUMMER

Spray
Spray everything with a diluted seaweed mixture.

Pruning
Cut the oldest blackcurrant stems back hard after harvesting the last of the fruit.

Plant
Transplant rooted strawberry runners.

Sow
Winter lettuces and salad plants
Japanese and spring onions
Winter spinach
Green manures as soil becomes vacant.

Grass
Cut the grass if needed.

JOBS TO DO

✔ Weed everything as needed.

✔ Retouch sticky bands.

✔ Inspect regularly for any sign of pests and diseases.

✔ Protect fruit and provide water for birds.

✔ Thin, harvest and use or preserve ripening fruits.

✔ Harvest and store potatoes and onions.

✔ Order hardy trees and shrubs for autumn planting.

✔ Clean, paint and repair timber, gutters and brickwork.

EARLY AUTUMN

Spray
Spray everything with a diluted seaweed mixture.

Pruning
Cut back herbaceous plants to 15 cm (6 in), as the stems start to wither. Remove old canes and tie in new for raspberries and blackberries.

Plant
Garlic and other bulbs

Sow *(under cover)*:
Winter lettuces and salad plants
Early carrots
Turnips
Chinese greens

(outside):
Green manures

Grass
Cut the grass if needed.

JOBS TO DO

✔ Weed everything as needed.

✔ Retouch sticky bands.

✔ Protect flowers, fruits and tender plants from early frosts.

✔ Harvest and use, store or preserve fruits and nuts.

✔ Make fruit juices, cider and wine with surplus fruit.

✔ Collect and dry seeds.

✔ Rake over old mulch.

✔ Take cuttings of most woody plants just before leaves drop.

✔ Check for pests and try to eliminate before winter.

MID-AUTUMN

Pruning

Prune late flowering shrubs, soft fruit and grapes
as the leaves fall. Cut back herbaceous plants
to 15 cm (6 in) as the stems start to wither.
Remove old canes and tie in new ones for
raspberries and blackberries.

Plant

Garlic and other bulbs.
Deciduous shrubs, trees and soft fruit.

Feed

Incorporate compost with all plantings.
Spread sieved compost around trees, shrubs and
soft fruit.

Mulch

Spread mulches under and around everything
possible.

Sow *(under cover)*:

Winter lettuces and salad plants
Summer cauliflower
Sweet peas
Green manures in greenhouse

Grass

Cut the grass weekly, raising height of mower
setting.

JOBS TO DO

✔ Weed everything as needed.

✔ Retouch sticky bands.

✔ Protect less hardy plants against frost, and move pots indoors.

✔ Put cloches over salad plants and autumn strawberries.

✔ Turn compost heaps and sieve for use or cover and store.

✔ Make new beds and borders, and move turf or stack and rot down.

✔ Lift and divide rhubarb.

✔ Harvest and use, store or preserve fruits and nuts.

✔ Collect and dry seeds and berries for seed and to feed to the birds.

LATE AUTUMN

Pruning
Prune late flowering shrubs, soft fruit and grapes as the leaves fall. Cut back herbaceous plants to 15 cm (6 in) as the stems start to wither. Rework and winter prune apples, pears and non-stone fruits.

Plant
Deciduous shrubs, trees and soft fruit.

Feed
Incorporate compost with all plantings.
Spread sieved compost on top of asparagus and globe artichokes.

Mulch
Spread mulches under and around everything possible.

Sow
Hardy peas
Broad beans
both for an extra early crop

Grass
Cut the grass if necessary.

JOBS TO DO

✔ Weed everything as needed.

✔ Retouch sticky bands.

✔ Order seed catalogues, potatoes and herbaceous plants for spring.

✔ Harvest and store last fruits and root vegetables in hard areas.

✔ Collect up all wastes for composting or shred for mulching.

EARLY WINTER

Pruning

Prune late flowering shrubs, soft fruit and grapes as the leaves fall.

Rework and winter-prune apples, pears and non-stone fruits.

Plant

Deciduous shrubs, trees and soft fruit.

Feed

Incorporate compost with all plantings.

Spread compost on top of crowns of herbaceous plants.

Grass

Lime the grass, aerate and spike if needed, adding sharp sand.

JOBS TO DO

✔ Weed everything as needed.

✔ Retouch sticky bands.

✔ Clean greenhouse, coldframe and cloche glass and plastic.

✔ Harvest and store root vegetables in milder areas.

✔ Check fruits in store.
  Plan for next year.

✔ Sit back, relax and enjoy what you have
  achieved this year.

CROP VALUES

Yields from a 3-metre (10-foot) row:

CROP	YIELD kg/lb	EASE OF GROWING		
		easy	moderate	hard
beans, broad	3.6/8	✗		
beans, french	5.9/13		✗	
beans, runner	9/20	✗		
beetroots	5.4/12		✗	
broccoli	2.7/6			✗
brussels sprouts	5.4/12		✗	
cabbages	4.5/10	✗		
cauliflowers	3.6/8			✗
carrots	5/11			✗
celery	4.5/10			✗
courgettes	4.5/10	✗		
cucumbers, ridge	4.5/10		✗	
garlics/shallots	3.6/8	✗		
kohl rabi	4/9	✗		
leeks	3.6/8			✗
lettuces	2.2/5		✗	
onions	4.5/10		✗	
parsnips	4/9		✗	
peas	2.6/7	✗		
potatoes	9/20	✗		
radishes	2.7/6		✗	
spinach	3.6/8		✗	
sweetcorn	2.2/5	✗		
tomatoes	9/20		✗	

| WORK REQUIRED | | | COST | |
a lot	moderate	little	expensive	cheap
		X	X	
	X		X	
X			X	
	X			X
	X			X
	X			X
	X			X
	X			X
X				X
X				X
		X		X
		X	X	
		X	X	
	X			X
	X			X
	X			X
X			X	
	X		X	
X			X	
	X		X	
		X		X
X				X
X			X	
X				X

CROP ROTATION

The importance of crop rotation cannot be overstressed. With crop rotation, vegetables in the same botanical family are grown in a different part of the garden each year. Crop rotation can improve soil fertility and help lessen the threat of pests and diseases that affect a specific plant family.

Vegetables in the same botanical family have similar nutrient requirements. In addition, there are those plants that actually improve the soil's structure and add nutrients. By alternating the planting of different types of crops, the health of the soil can be maintained. Crop rotation plans should cover at least three years, but remember the longer the better.

For a four-year rotation plan you could:
Divide the available land into four sections, and plant potatoes in one, legumes in the next, brassicas in another and roots in the last. The next year, move them all along one strip, and repeat each year. By the fifth year the crops should be in the same position as the first year.

1st year	spuds	legumes	greens	roots
2nd year	legumes	greens	roots	spuds
3rd year	greens	roots	spuds	legumes
4th year	roots	spuds	legumes	greens
5th year	spuds	legumes	greens	roots

Dig a good amount of well-rotted manure into the soil into which the potatoes are to be planted.

Roots could be:
Beetroot, carrot, Jerusalem artichoke, parsnip, salsify, scorzonera.
Do not add manure or lime before this crop.

Greens could be:
Broccoli, brussels sprout, cabbage, cauliflower, kale, kohl rabi, radish, swede, turnip.
Make sure the soil is limed if it needs it.

Legumes are pea and bean crops.
Add a liberal amount of well-rotted manure or compost at digging time.
Lime only if the soil is known to be acid.

A few rules to bear in mind:
• Plant brassicas and leafy greens to follow legumes
  — they like the added nitrogen;
• Legumes follow a manured crop;
• Never manure carrots or parsnips;
• Group crops according to which diseases they are susceptible to;
• Never repeat any crop with a crop of the same type within four years, make it longer if possible;
• Any plot that has suffered from severe clubroot should be given as long as possible before brassicas are grown again.

LUNAR GARDENING

Before you turn the page and think that I have gone mad, you might like to know that the Moon influences more than just ocean tides. It has long been documented that a Full Moon affects the behaviour of humans and animals — so why not plants, too?

Lunar gardening has been passed down through many generations. Today, there are many believers in lunar gardening who will not plant anything unless a favourable Moon is indicated. It centres on the Moon's gravitational effect on the flow of moisture in both the soil and plants.

As mentioned earlier, the Moon not only controls the tides but it also influences the water table — the level at which the ground water pressure is equal to atmospheric pressure — and also the movement of fluids in plants. The basis of lunar gardening is understanding the effects of the Moon, and calculating your gardening chores accordingly. For example, by only mowing your lawn on certain days, might mean that you could mow less often. Also, it is believed that the best time to turn over garden soil is during the last quarter of the Moon, because that is when the water table has dropped to its lowest point. This means that there is less moisture in the soil.

USING THE MOON'S PHASES

The lunar month starts with the New Moon. From the New Moon to the first quarter, and from the first quarter to the Full Moon, the Moon appears to us to change shape. For example we see it as a crescent which gradually increases during the month to become a Full Moon.

Chores to do by the light of the Moon:
• Repot and tend houseplants;
• Sow seeds of plants that grow above ground;
• Fertilise;
• Graft fruit trees;
• Plant evergreen and deciduous trees.

Chores to do by the dark of the Moon:
• Plant bulbs;
• Plant crops that grow below ground, such as potatoes and carrots;
• Plant biennials and perennials because they need strong roots;
• Eliminate slugs;
• Prune shrubs — as the Moon starts to wane during the 3rd and 4th quarters, this is a good time to prune plants, as the water table is diminishing and there will be less sap to flow out of the cut ends.

Go on, have a go yourself. See what difference it makes to your garden by using the power of the Moon.

PESTS, DISEASES AND WEEDS

PREVENTION IS BETTER THAN CURE

There are many options if you have a pest, disease or pernicious weed problem and do not care about polluting your planet, local ecosystem and even the health of you and your family. Simply visit your local DIY or garden centre and pick up one of the many chemicals available to fix nearly any ill that may afflict your garden.

To the organic gardener — the gardener who cares about his environment — there are also a few options available for off-the-shelf remedies that are acceptable to deal with problems once they have occurred; but it is far better to prevent these troubles happening in the first place. Your first step to healthy plants is to provide them with the best possible growing conditions; in this way you are helping them withstand minor infestations. Work the soil so that it supplies the required nutrients, and has the correct structure and moisture content that the plant requires. Finally, position plants in the correct amount of shade or light in temperatures in which they are known to do well.

If you cannot provide the conditions the plant requires it may be a better option to consider growing an alternative plant. For example, do not try to grow rhododendron on chalky soil, and don't expect to grow good carrots on heavy soil. It is good to experiment and try your luck with new plants but have a backup in case of failure.

For example, seeds of crop varieties popular in Italy have started to become easily available in the UK. If you wish to try growing one of the Italian types of tomato grow a few tried and trusted moneymaker or gardener's delight plants as well — just in case you have a typical British summer and not the fluke Mediterranean one you wish for.

Use plant varieties that are resistant to pest and disease. For example, try blight-resistant potatoes such as 'Remarka' and 'Sarpo', and root aphid resistant lettuce such as 'Milan'. Good seed catalogues usually list pest and disease resistant qualities of the varieties available.

Good hygiene in the garden is a very important part of keeping pest, disease and disorder to a minimum. Regularly inspect all parts of the garden and act swiftly to remove any pest or infected material. For example, if you see white butterflies lay eggs on the underside of cabbage leaves simply wipe them off with a damp cloth. Remove or burn infected plant material as soon as possible in order to keep the problem under control. Then make sure you clean and sterilise any secateurs, knives and saws used to remove the infected material.

By following good husbandry and well-founded and trusted techniques, you should be successful in growing healthy plants that will fend off pest, disease and disorder.

In short:

- Work the soil to provide the best possible growing conditions.

- Provide the plant with the correct amount of water.

- Use mulches.

- Inspect plants regularily for signs of pests and disease and deal with the problem promptly. Burn or bury diseased plants.

- When buying plants examine carefully, and reject any with signs of disease.

- Do not overcrowd plants, especially seedlings.

- Sow seedlings in sterilized compost.

- Clean tools and sterilize after using them to deal with infected material.

- Use companion planting, physical barriers and intercropping to confuse pests in the vegetable garden.

- Use crop rotation where appropriate.

- Use biological controls.

COMPANION PLANTING

Companion planting is a very simple, easy and widely acknowledged way of protecting one plant by using a certain quality of another. It should be part of every organic gardener's arsenal of weapons to keep problems at bay. Its simplest form, for an example, could be providing shelter from sun or wind by using another plant. Leafy ground cover under clematis keeps roots cool and moist, which are ideal growing conditions.

Companion plants can improve the vigour of other plants: often legumes are used to fix nitrogen. White clover, for example, is included in some grass seed mixes for this reason. Green manure can be regarded as a form of companion planting and more information on this is provided in the chapter on soil.

Some plants exude chemicals or strong scents from their roots or foliage which can deter pests: African Marigolds repel nematodes so it makes a good companion plant for root crops which are attacked by nematodes. Similarly, plant scents can be used to attract beneficial insects into the garden and also sacrificial plants can be used to attract pests away from other plants: nasturtiums attract black fly away from other plants such as beans.

Some plants make bad neighbours because they compete for the same nutrients or exude incompatible chemicals or strong aromas.

Some of the best companions include:

ALLIUMS such as onions, garlic, leeks, shallots and chives deter aphids and carrot fly. Intercropping onions and leeks with carrots confuses both carrot and onion flies. Chives help overcome black spot and increase rose perfume.

BASIL is good planted with tomatoes to improve growth and flavour and to repel flies.

BORAGE attracts bees, accumulates minerals for the compost heap and grows well with strawberries.

CARROTS can be used to disguise the smell of the allium family of plants to deter onion fly and leak moth.

CELERY deters cabbage white caterpillars from brassicas.

CHERVIL keeps aphids off lettuce and aids radishes.

CORIANDER repels aphids and can be made into a spray to repel red spider mite.

FOXGLOVES attract beneficial insects especially bees, and are believed to stimulate the growth of plants. They accumulate a high level of minerals in the leaves which are good for the compost heap.

MARIGOLDS, AFRICAN (*Tagetes erecta*), MEXICAN (*T. minuta*) and FRENCH (*Tagetes patula*) are excellent for controlling nematodes (eelworms). Plant dense areas of them for the best effect. Studies show that this nematode killing effect lasts for several years. These marigolds also help to deter whiteflies when planted around tomatoes and can be used in greenhouses for the same purpose. *Tagetes minuta* inhibits ground-elder, couch grass and some other weeds, but may also inhibit the growth of some herbs.

MARIGOLDS, COMMON OR POT (*Calendula officinalis*) are said to repel pests from tomatoes, can lure aphids away from beans and deters asparagus beetles. It attracts beneficial predators to the plot such as ladybirds, lacewings and hoverflies. This can be used as a sacrificial plant to lure slugs away from lettuce.

NASTURTIUMS work as a decoy to lure blackfly away from other plants. Conversely, nasturtiums deter aphids and pests of the curcurbit family. Studies say this is among the best at attracting predatory insects. Woolly aphids can be repelled from apple trees by planting nasturtiums around the base of the tree.

PEAS and other legumes like sweet peas and lupins are known for their ability to fix nitrogen: they convert nitrogen, by way of bacteria that live in the roots, into a form that can be used easily by other plants. Plant a few sweet peas amongst french and runner beans to attract pollinating insects.

POACHED EGG PLANT (*Limnanthes douglasii*) is a great attraction for bees and hoverflies.

ROSEMARY is a good companion to cabbage, beans, carrots and sage. It deters cabbage moths, bean beetles, and carrot flies.

SAGE hides the smell of brassicas and carrots and confuses pests.

TANSY is used to deter flying insects and ants.

WORMWOOD is a cabbage butterfly and moth repellent, and deters cats and other animals.

ORGANIC PESTICIDE TREATMENTS

A few chemical treatments are made from natural sources and are tolerable for use in an organic garden. This does not mean, however, that all chemicals made from natural sources are acceptable. In the UK and Europe legislation restricts the sale and use of pesticides. Organic or not, if it kills chemically rather than physically, then an approval is needed before products can be used, and this applies to both homemade and 'off the shelf' treatments.

I provide information on treatments that are, and have been used as, pesticides in various parts of the world. Some have been proved to be harmful and have been banned from use; others are harmful and are still available; some are relatively benign and acceptable to use. You should confirm that any pesticides you use are allowed by the relevent laws and legislation, and these vary widely between countries and are subject to constant review and revision.

BORDEAUX MIXTURE is a fungicidal suspension of copper sulphate and lime. Although it is an inorganic chemical, it is allowed by many organic standards. It was used first in Bordeaux, France, to control downy mildew, hence its name. Bordeaux mixture is primarily a fungicide that controls bacterial leaf spots, blights, downy mildews and cankers. It also repels many insects. The compound is used on many vegetables, tree fruits and nut crops. It is a preventative, not a cure, and must be applied thoroughly in good time.

ELDER SPRAY is an organic spray used as a pesticide and fungicide based on *Sambucus nigra* the Common Elder. Chop up 1 kg (2 lb) elder leaves and soak for 24 hours in 10 litres (2.5 gallons) of water and then boil for 30 minutes. Allow to cool and strain. Spray undiluted against aphids, beetles and caterpillars. The use of Elder spray as a pesticide is allowed under current EU legislation. Horseradish, ginger, rhubarb leaves, garlic and chilli have also been used in home-made organic pesticides.

CHILLI BASED PESTICIDES can be used against a variety of pests. They will kill ants, aphids, caterpillars, grubs, bugs and just about anything small, so it is important to be selective. The chilli acts as an antifeedant, poison and repellant. There are a number of different recipes available and in addition to chilli, ingredients may include garlic, mexican marigold, soft soap and onion. Be careful with regard to the strength of the mixture, as plants can easily be burnt if it is too strong. Experiment with it if necessary and check for results or any damage to young plants. If it fixes the problem and your plants are happy you've got the perfect mix, but if there's still pests then lower the water dilution rate or change the ingredient quantities slightly. It's best to spray every few days until there's no sign of pests; then about every week to 10 days for any eggs or larvae that may have hatched out.

One recipe is known as garlic fire spray:

2—3 garlic bulbs
6 large or 12 smaller hot chilli peppers
1 tablespoon vegetable oil
3 tsp soft soap
1½ litres water

Blend a third of the water and all of the other ingredients into a liquidiser, then strain through muslin, a coffee filter or similar, and add the remaining water. Pour what you need into a spray bottle for use and keep the rest in a well-labeled air and water tight container. This spray is also worth trying as a repellent against larger pests like rabbits.

DERRIS is a pesticide that was once very popular with organic gardeners and was used to control smaller insects especially mites, aphids, sawflies and also wasps. It is sometimes referred to as rotenone. It could be called a natural substance because it is derived from a climbing leguminous plant from Southeast Asia. Derris is NOT harmless and is now banned, or about to be banned, in many countries. For a long time derris has been known to be lethal to tortoises, pigs and fish. Some New Guinea natives practise a form of fishing in which they crush the roots of the derris plants and throw them into the water. The stunned or killed fish float to the surface where they can be easily reached. Some studies have linked long-term exposure to derris/rotenone in laboratory animals with symptoms associated with Parkinson's disease.

NEEM is a botanical pesticide derived from the neem tree, a native of India. Neem has been used for more than 4,000 years for medicinal and pest control purposes in India and Africa. It is not highly toxic to mammals. Neem supplies at least two compounds, azadirachtin and salannin, that have insecticidal properties and other unknown compounds with fungicidal properties. Products containing extracts from the seeds have been developed for sale as commercial insecticides and are available in some parts of the world, but are not allowed under current UK legislation.

PYRETHRUM is made from the flowerheads of chrysanthemums. Although a natural product, it is no longer regarded as a safe insecticide by most organic growers. While it is relatively benign to mammals (it can be a skin irritant and sensitiser) it is very dangerous to insects because of its wide-spectrum action. It can kill as many good insects as it does pest species — bees for instance. Even in places where it is available and legal to use, a substitute with safer characteristics is now recommended.

SOFT SOAP is a safe and effective insecticide to control aphids, brassica whitefly and cabbage white caterpillars. For best results, drench the insects thoroughly using a powerful sprayer taking care to avoid beneficial insects like bees, ladybirds or lacewings. It is a contact insecticide which will only kill what it hits. The fatty acids disrupt the structure and permeability of the insect cell membranes. There is no benefit in spraying parts of the plant not infected. Use pure liquid soaps and not washing up detergents.

SULPHUR on its own is a fungicide favoured by organic gardeners, as it is safe for people and for the environment, because it is an essential plant nutrient. Take care when using it on some fruit trees and bushes as some varieties do not react well to sulphur. It is used to control powdery mildew on fruit, flowers and vegetables and for preventing rots in overwintering bulbs and tubers.

BIOLOGICAL CONTROLS

This technique uses one living organism to control another with no danger of harm to humans, the environment and beneficial creatures. The introduced organisms range from predatory insects to much smaller single cell pathogenic bacteria and viruses. Controls are usually supplied by mail order: being living animals with limited lives they cannot normally be stocked in shops. The exceptions are the nematodes used against slugs, vine weevil larvae, chafer grubs, leatherjackets and some other pests. These may be stocked in refrigerated cabinets in some garden centres.

Pests that can be attacked by biological controls include:

APHIDS — Ladybird larvae are an effective predator for the control of aphids in the greenhouse environment. Apply when temperatures have reached 10 degrees.

CHAFER GRUBS — The nematode (*Heterorhabditis megidis*) should be applied during September while the young chafer grubs are active.

RED SPIDER MITE — Start control as soon as the mites are detected by applying *Phytoseiulus persimilis*. These predatory mites are capable of devouring large numbers of the spider mites and breed very rapidly. The persimilis mite is effective at a wide temperature range, from 4 to 28°C, and can also be used outdoors.

SLUGS — The nematode, *Phasmarhabditis hermaphrodita*, attacks slugs and occurs naturally in the soil. Their numbers can be boosted by introducing more at the beginning of the growing season in March and April.

VINE WEEVIL — Treat plants with *Steinernema kraussei* (a nematode) when the vine weevil larvae are active in early Spring and Autumn. The nematodes need a minimum soil temperature of 5°C.

WHITEFLY — The parasitic wasp, *Encarsia formosa* is a very effective way to control whitefly, supplied as pupae on cards which are hung in a shady position throughout the crop. Whitefly control will be most effective when temperatures are at least 18°C during the day and 14°C at night. Whitefly need to be present before the control can be introduced.

As well as insects and nematodes, larger animals can be considered as beneficial and are in effect also biological controls.

Some plants and crops need to be protected from birds, but on the whole they should be encouraged as they eat far more pests than they do crops. So provide good habitats, nests boxes, feed and water.

Frogs and toads eat pests, especially slugs. Entice amphibians to your garden by creating a wildlife pond with shallow sloping edges planted with moisture-loving plants.

Hedgehogs love to eat slugs! If you have the room keep a corner of your garden a little bit wild to provide suitable habitat for hedgehogs. If you think your area is suitable for hedgehogs yet you do not appear to have any, it may be worth contacting a local hedgehog care centre who could possibly use your garden as a release site for rehabilitated hedgehogs. Never use slug pellets as these are harmful to hedgehogs.

TRAPS, BARRIERS AND PHYSICAL CONTROL OF PESTS

Barrier methods of pest control consist of physically separating the pest from its food source. They are an effective and safe way of preventing a pest problem. The pest may be actually removed physically from the threatened plants, as in removing snails or picking caterpillars off cabbage; or the pest may be excluded by netting or by fencing. Scaring may be effective too.

Physical control does not interfere with other natural control systems which is a major advantage. It may be more expensive and time-consuming than chemical control but there are no harmful residues to consider. The removal of old crops and debris that harbour pests is an important part of physical control, as is early digging to expose overwintering pests to the weather, and to predators.

Barriers and traps are a preventative measure and should be put in place before the problem arises. Flying pests can be kept out by netting. Make sure that you choose the right mesh size for the pest involved. Carrots can be grown under fleece to protect them against carrot root fly.

Use plastic bottles, with the tops removed and bottoms cut off, as mini-cloches to protect young plants from slugs and caterpillars.

A 12 cm (5 in) square piece of kitchen foil, or some other material, fitted as a collar around the base of cabbages as soon as they are planted will help protect against cabbage rootfly.

WARNING: don't waste beer in traps for slugs! The beer trap, so beloved of organic gardeners, actually kills more beneficial creatures than slugs! So you are advised to drink all your beer. Make barriers from plastic bottles by cutting 10 cm (4 in) deep rings from them to make slug barriers for individual plants. These need to be buried at least 1 cm ($\frac{1}{2}$ in) deep in the soil, but are very effective at keeping slugs out until the plants have grown enough to be able to withstand a little slug damage.

Bright yellow sticky card traps can be hung in a greenhouse to attract pests such as adult whitefly and sciarid flies. No pesticides are involved, but monitor the traps to ensure beneficial insects are not being trapped. Remove before introducing the predators *encarsia formosa*.

Grease can be painted as a band around mature fruit trees to act as a barrier against winter moth and ants. Apply in autumn and then again in the spring.

Pick off pests and infected leaves by hand when you see them. Never allow problems to take hold.

Birds can be kept off crops and plants by placing netting on them. Specific plastic netting is available, or chicken wire can be used. Floating cloches, fleece and enviromesh, used mainly to protect from frost and insect damage, will also protect from bird damage. Use cages over fruit.

Make bird scarers — try CDs and aluminium foil reflective streamers that spin and flutter when the wind blows. Get the kids to make scarecrows!

PESTS

APHIDS

Aphids (blackfly and greenfly) are one of the most common and troublesome of all garden insects, and cause damage by feeding on the sap of young shoots.

SYMPTOMS: Clusters of small, variously coloured, round-bodied insects on leaves and stems. Distortion of young growth and galls or sticky honeydew on foliage.

PREVENTION: Encourage insects that feed on aphids. Plant companion plants like tagetes, calendula and poached egg plants to attract hoverflies, ladybirds and lacewings.

TREATMENT: Aphids breathe through their skin, so spraying them with a solution of soft/insecticidal soap blocks the pores and they suffocate.

Encourage the natural predators of aphids including lacewings and ladybirds. You can obtain these as biological controls via mail-order. The eggs are placed on the plant, near to where the infestation is. Both larvae and adults will consume many aphids in one day.

ASPARAGUS BEETLE

These little bugs are about 6 mm (¼ in) long, and are black with yellow spots.

SYMPTOMS: Stem damage causes brown patches on foliage.

PREVENTION: These beetles overwinter in plant debris near asparagus beds, so keep these areas clear. Rake over and disturb areas that are likely to habour the bugs from time to time.

TREATMENT: They can be picked off individually in most cases, but if they become too numerous spray with pyrethrum as a last resort, while being careful to avoid harming beneficial organisms. Derris was the treatment favoured by organic gardeners, but is no longer advised because of the fear of harm to health and the environment.

BEAN SEED FLY
Small white maggots eat into the germinating seeds of beans, peas, sweetcorn and other vegetables.

SYMPTOMS: Brown depressed areas on the cotyledons and growing point of the seedlings.

PREVENTION: Seeds that are slow to germinate are especially vulnerable. Covering plantings with fleece will help warm up the soil to speed up germination, while also providing a physical barrier. Alternatively sow seeds in modules and start off indoors to be planted out later.

BLACKCURRANT GALL MITE

This is the most serious blackcurrant pest not only for the direct damage done but because it transmits reversion virus.

SYMPTOMS: Buds swell and then fail to develop.

TREATMENT: Remove and burn infested buds.

CABBAGE ROOT FLY

The maggots of this fly attack the roots of recently transplanted cabbages and other brassicas.

SYMPTOMS: Young plants collapse.

PREVENTION: Prevention of cabbage root fly can be achieved by placing a 15 cm (6 in) diameter collar of thick cardboard around each plant. This will prevent the fly from laying eggs on the soil near the plant. There is no organic way of treating affected plants other than to dig them all up and burn them.

CABBAGE WHITEFLY

Common pest of all brassicas; often active in winter.

SYMPTOMS: Small whiteflies take flight from the underside of leaves when disturbed. Leaves are discoloured and sticky and plant growth is checked.

TREATMENT: First try spraying with soft soap or a chilli based pesticide; if this does not work use pyrethrum.

CAPSID BUGS

A wide range of plants, including currants and gooseberries, are affected by several species of green bug which is about 6mm ($^{1}/_{4}$ in) long with six long legs and antennae.

SYMPTOMS: Ragged holes in leaves, and misshapen and discoloured fruits.

PREVENTION: Good garden hygiene.

CARROT FLY

Maggots burrow into roots of carrots, parsnips, parsley and celery. Female carrot flies are attracted by the smell released when plantings are thinned.

SYMPTOMS: Young plants die off, and mature roots are spoiled by tunnels.

PREVENTION: Cover the plants with a horticultural fleece or mesh, or surround them with 60 cm (2 ft) high barriers made of clear polythene to exclude the low-flying female flies. Carrot cultivars such as 'Maestro', 'Resistafly' and 'Sytan' are less susceptible to carrot fly. Use companion plants that disguise the smell of carrots, such as onions and sage.

CATERPILLARS

There are many types of caterpillar that attack plants. Most eat leaves but some eat roots, stems or fruit. Brassicas are the most affected and this is usually by the larval stage of the small cabbage white butterfly.

SYMPTOMS: Ragged holes in leaves, and plants may be destroyed.

PREVENTION: Protect the plants with horticultural fleece or mesh. Use companion plantings of rosemary and/or wormwood.

TREATMENT: Spray young caterpillars as they hatch with the biological control *Steinernema carpocapsae*, or remove and squash the caterpillars by hand when they are young and still on the outer leaves.

CELERY FLY/LEAF MINER
Maggots burrow or 'mine' into the leaves of celery and parsnips.

SYMPTOMS: Checked growth or death of plants, and brown blotches on leaves.

TREATMENT: Remove and burn affected leaves. Growing under fleece or fine mesh will help prevent attack.

CODLING MOTH
Codling moths cause more damage to apples than any other pest. May also attack pears and other fruits. Adult codling moths lay eggs in midsummer

in leaves or fruit. The caterpillars that emerge from these eggs tunnel into fruit and feed for several weeks.

SYMPTOMS: 'Maggoty' fruit, with hollow, brown and rotted cores.

PREVENTION AND TREATMENT: Maggots can not be treated once they have entered the fruit so this must be prevented.

Nematodes (*Steinernema carpocapsae*) can be used to control the overwintering pupae on trees and in the ground from September. The nematodes are applied with a sprayer during the evenings or on dull days.

Codling moth pheromone traps will not control codling moths, but on isolated trees it may catch enough males to reduce the females' mating success, and so resulting in fewer maggots. The traps consists of an open-sided box that is hung in the tree in early May. The bottom of the box has a sticky sheet on which the pheromone pellet is placed; this exudes a scent similar to that produced by female codling moth. Male moths are lured into the trap and get stuck. By counting the trapped males every week, and following the instructions that come with the trap, you can monitor the threat.

Females laying eggs and maggots on trees making their way to fruit can be sprayed with a soft soap solution, or picked off and destroyed.

CUTWORMS

The name given to various caterpillars that attack a range of plants including lettuces and root vegetables. They are stout, soft-bodied and smooth, and curl up tightly when disturbed. They can be dull grey, brown, or black, and may be striped or spotted.

SYMPTOMS: The stems of young plants are eaten at, or just above, ground level and are sometimes completely severed.

TREATMENT: Spraying or watering around the affected plants with a preparation made from pyrethrum, chilli or garlic can be effective against cutworms. Search out and destroy the grubs at first sign of attack.

FLEA BEETLE

A pest of young brassicas, radishes, swedes and turnips.

SYMPTOMS: Young leaves are pitted with very small holes.

PREVENTION: Good garden hygiene. Flea beetles go for seedlings which are lacking water. The best prevention therefore is to keep seedlings sufficiently watered in dry conditions.

FRIT FLY
A serious pest of sweetcorn seedlings.

SYMPTOMS: Striped and tattered leaves which may cause stunted growth and the central tip to die.

PREVENTION: This pest is only a threat in late May and early July, so protect plants with cloches or fine mesh at this time. Keep plants sown indoors in the greenhouse until the threat has passed.

GREENHOUSE WHITEFLY
Affects greenhouse tomatoes and cucumbers.

SYMPTOMS: Small whiteflies take off from underside of leaves when disturbed. Leaves are discoloured and plant growth checked.

PREVENTION: Most types of marigolds are repellent to whiteflies.

TREATMENT: Spray insects with diluted soft soap or chilli based spray. The predator wasp, *Encarsia formosa*, is a widely available biological control. Use a mini, battery powered vacuum cleaner to hoover the pests up!

GOOSEBERRY SAWFLY

Various species of sawfly caterpillar cause severe damage to gooseberries and currants.

SYMPTOMS: Light green caterpillars with black spots strip leaves from plants. The first sign of damage will be noticed at the base of the bushes.

PREVENTION: Regularly check the plants for sawfly from mid-April onwards and pick off the larvae by hand.

TREATMENT: Spray when young larvae are seen with pyrethrum.

LEAF EELWORM

Attacks strawberries and other soft fruits.

SYMPTOMS: Symptoms are seen mainly in damp summers and autumns. The foliage becomes yellow and eventually brownish-black.

PREVENTION: Remove and burn affected leaves.

LEAFHOPPERS

Related to aphids, these bugs feed on the sap of a wide range of plants, both indoor and out.

SYMPTOMS: There is yellow to white mottling of upper surface of leaves; whole leaves may become puckered and turn brown at the edges. Green insects leap from the underside of disturbed foliage.

TREATMENT: Cover a piece of stiff card with grease or a sticky glue and hold it near the infected plants while lightly brushing the leaves with your other hand. The disturbed insects should become stuck to the card and this can then be disposed of.

Neem-based sprays are said to be effective against leafhoppers where they are permitted to be used.

The parasytical wasp *Anagrus atomus* can be used as biological control.

LEATHERJACKETS

The larvae of craneflies (daddy-longlegs) feed on the roots of a wide range of plants. They can cause severe damage to lawns.

SYMPTOMS: From April to June these grey-brown, legless grubs are found on soil. Plants wilt and sometimes die, and lawns develop yellow patches where the roots have been eaten. In severe cases the turf can be pulled up easily to reveal no roots! Secondary damage from birds and animals is just as destructive, as they often dig up lawns looking for the grubs to eat.

PREVENTION: Before planting dig deeply to expose grubs to birds.

TREATMENT: A nematode: biological control is available and must be applied between August and October.

MEALY BUG
A serious greenhouse pest.

SYMPTOMS: Stunted foliage is covered with patches of waxy thread. Usually you can see the insects themselves and their yellow egg clusters. Mealy bugs don't like light, so look for them on the undersides of leaves and stems. They attack at any time of year, but mainly late summer and autumn.

TREATMENT: Spray with soft/insecticidal soap solution. Expect the mealy bugs to resist treatment — they're protected by a waterproof wax — however, the soap can break that down if done repeatedly.

MILLIPEDES
Pest of root crops, bulbs and tubers, strawberries and in greenhouses. Do not confuse with centipedes which are beneficial. Millipedes are grey-black in colour, have a greater number of legs, and are slower than centipedes.

SYMPTOMS: Tunnels in potatoes and other root crops.

PREVENTION: Millipedes feed mainly on decaying plant material, and therefore clear away and compost rotting vegetation. Keep strawberries off the soil by placing straw under them.

ONION EEL WORM
Affects onions, shallots and garlic.

SYMPTOMS: Swollen leaves, stems and bulbs occur during June, July and August.

PREVENTION: Crop rotation plan. Give a plot 2—3 years before growing onions and related crops on it again. Dig up and burn infested plants.

ONION FLY
A significant pest of onions, leeks and shallots.

SYMPTOMS: Mushy bulbs with small white maggots feeding on them. The flies look very similar to houseflies.

PREVENTION: Cover sowings made before May with fleece, and those after that with insect-proof mesh, to protect against onion fly. Use companion plants to disguise and hide the scent of onions; sow thinly and avoid thinning onion seedlings if possible.

PEA MOTH
Maggots found in peas are in fact the caterpillars of this small moth.

SYMPTOMS: Tiny, pale yellow caterpillars found eating peas in the pods.

PREVENTION: Grow early maturing varieties that will crop before the pest is starts activity in June. For small areas of peas, cover the crop with fine mesh during the period from flowering until the pods are at least half filled.

POTATO CYST EELWORM

A serious pest of potatoes and tomatoes. There are different types of cyst eelworm and they are regional. The golden cyst eelworm predominates in southern Britain, while the white cyst eelworm is more common north of Yorkshire and Lancashire.

SYMPTOMS: Tiny cysts about 1mm in diameter appear on roots and cause wilting and death of plants. When the cysts first develop they are white in both species. Those of the white cyst eelworm then turn brown; those of the golden cyst eelworm go through a pale yellow phase before they also become brown. The eggs within can remain viable for years which makes re-infection almost inevitable.

PREVENTION: Use crop rotation. Avoid planting tomatoes and potatoes in the same space for as many growing seasons as you can to reduce the threat. A heavily infested soil may need six or seven potato-free years before you can safely replant it.

Use resistant potato cultivars. 'Pentland Javelin', 'Maris Piper', 'Rocket', and 'Swift', are resistant to white cyst eelworm. 'Kestrel', 'Sante' and 'Valor' have some resistance to both white and golden cyst eelworm.

RED SPIDER MITES

A serious pest, not only of greenhouse crops but also cucumbers and strawberries, that loves hot and dry conditions.

SYMPTOMS: Mottling of upper leaf surfaces, yellowing of plant and silky webs on underside of leaves.

PREVENTION: Keep greenhouses humid, and it is also worth spraying outdoor plants with cold water.

TREATMENT: In greenhouses introduce the predatory mite *Phytoselius persimilis*. This can also be used on outdoor plants from May to August.

SLUGS AND SNAILS

Most gardeners' number one enemy!

SYMPTOMS: Large holes in foliage, tubers and roots eaten. Slime trails are often found.

TREATMENT: Slug pellets containing metaldehyde and/or methiocarb are poisonous to mammals and must not be used.

Parasitic nematodes supplied in granule form, can be mixed in a watering can and applied to the garden. The slugs normally die underground so there is no slimy mess to be seen. The Nematodes work when the soil is at least 5°C/41°F and damp. An application twice a year should be sufficient.

PREVENTION: Encourage hedgehogs, frogs and toads to visit your garden.

Use barriers, such as collars cut from plastic bottles to put around young plants. Use sharp materials like grit, ash and broken eggshells as mulches around threatened plants.

Collect the slugs by hand and transfer them to container of salt water. This is best done in the evening, so you will need a torch to spot them. Search the lawn, paths and around tasty plants. It is the little grey and white slugs that damage plants; the big black and brown ones are useful scavengers!

WIREWORM

These beetle larvae feed on the tubers, roots and stems of potatoes, tomatoes and lettuces.

SYMPTOMS: Golden brown, worm-like creatures, that are found among plant roots. They are tough skinned with three pairs of small legs located behind the head.

Small entry holes of 2—3 mm across are seen on the outside of corms, tubers or roots. A network of tunnels may be evident inside; these are often invaded and enlarged by other pests such as slugs or woodlice. Stems of seedlings bitten through at, or below, soil level. Roots may show small blackened pits where feeding has occurred; plants may suddenly wilt and die.

PREVENTION: Thorough cultivation before planting and after harvesting will help to expose the wireworm to natural predators such as birds, frogs and hedgehogs.

TREATMENT: The biological control *Heterorhabditis megadis* will attack wireworms. It is applied through a watering can in May—August, or as soon as the soil temp is 12°C and wireworms are present, with plenty of water applied afterwards so the nematodes can swim in the soil water to find the wireworms.

WOOLLY APHID

A common pest of apple, pear, prunus, pyracantha, cotoneaster, elm, hawthorn and mountain ash, usually appearing in spring.

SYMPTOMS: The adults are about 2mm long and a pinkish-brown colour, although they appear to be white with their waxy protection. As with all aphids they feed off plant sap, but their action causes a callous-like lump or gall to grow, which provides better access to the plant. These galls remain after infestation has gone.

PREVENTION: Encourage hoverflies, lacewings and ladybirds. Check susceptible plants regularly for infestations and treat pruning cuts with a wound sealant to remove this source of sap.

TREATMENT: Colonies can be rubbed away with a brush and soft soap solution. Soft soap solution can also be sprayed on the pest. A forceful jet of water will remove the bulk of a colony. Where allowed and obtainable, an organic spray made from extract of Neem called Azadiractin is effective.

DISEASES

ANTHRACNOSE

A fungal disease of beans.

SYMPTOMS: Brown, sunken marks develop on the pods, and leaves and stems may develop brown spots.

PREVENTION: Rotate crops. Bear in mind leguminous green manures may harbour bean diseases.

TREATMENT: Infected plants should be removed and destroyed immediately. Grow resistant cultivars, such as 'Aramis'.

APPLE CANKER

This fungus attacks the trunks and branches of apple trees and sometimes pear trees. Also known as fungal canker.

SYMPTOMS: Sunken, swollen, distorted and cracked areas of bark that may be dotted with small white or red pustules. Early symptoms include dead, leafless twigs or shoots bearing small sickly-looking leaves.

PREVENTION: Where possible, prevent and avoid scars or wounds caused by pruning, frost damage, scab and woolly aphids as the fungus enters the tree through these types of injury. Trees suffering from some other form of stress, for example, waterlogging or nutrient deficiency, are also more prone to the disease. Apple varieties 'Grenadier,

'Annie Elizabeth', 'Laxton's Superb', 'Newton Wonder', 'Lane's Prince Albert' or 'Winston', are resistant to canker.

TREATMENT: Prune out cankers on small branches and twigs. On larger areas you can remove the canker with a sharp knife or chisel. Make sure that you cut back well into healthy wood; apply canker paint to the cut areas, and destroy all infected tissue. Avoid pruning in wet weather.

BACTERIAL CANKER
Bacterial canker is a serious tree disease of almonds, cherries, nectarines, peaches and plums.

SYMPTOMS: In autumn shallow depressions are found at the base of branches. These enlarge in spring and completely circle the base of the branch causing it to die. An amber like gum may also appear.

PREVENTION: Pruning of the types of trees threatened by bacterial canker should be carried out in dry weather between June and August. When pruning out canker-affected branches, wipe the pruning tool with disinfectant between each cut.

TREATMENT: Spray the foliage, branches and trunk thoroughly with Bordeaux mixture to protect leaf scars and bark wounds from infection. Three applications of the fungicide are necessary at monthly intervals from about mid-August to mid-October.

BLACK LEG

Common disease of potatoes.

SYMPTOMS: Slimy black lesion appears at the base of the stem leading to collapse of the foliage; this then spreads to the tubers which rot if badly affected. Lightly contaminated tubers may appear healthy at lifting, but can then go on to rot during storage (this will then spread to adjacent tubers).

PREVENTION: The bacterium that causes black leg spreads from contaminated seed to infect young stems. The problem is more severe in wet soils. To reduce the risk of black leg use good quality, certified seed tubers, and improve drainage in wet soils.

TREATMENT: If one or two plants develop the disease ensure that these are dug up and destroyed as soon as possible.

BLOSSOM END ROT

Damage to tomato, pepper and aubergine fruits caused by calcium deficiency which is usually the result of irregular watering.

SYMPTOMS: Brown or black patches at the blossom end of the fruits.

PREVENTION: Don't allow the soil around the plant's roots to dry out. Water plants regularly as even a short period of drought can encourage the problem. Grow bags may be a better growing medium as they should contain sufficient calcium for a good crop of fruits. Never apply fertiliser to dry soil; always give plants plenty of water first. Make sure acid soil is limed prior to planting affected crops.

BOLTING

Bolting is the term used for premature flowering and often affects lettuces, endives and Chinese cabbages, as well as other crops.

SYMPTOMS: Plant shoots out flowering stem before crop develops properly. Any leaves are usually bitter.

PREVENTION: Bolting is usually caused by plants being put under stress: in particular climatic stress. So temperature plays a vital role. In early spring plants prefer cold nights and warm days. If the days are cold too then bolting is likely. Mild autumns and winters will also trigger this condition in certain crops. The factors are quite complex, and vary not only between crops, but even between different cultivars. Careful selection of cultivars and sowing dates can help limit the problem. Successional sowings will also help to achieve a constant supply of crops if the season is changeable. Dry soil can also encourage bolting, particularly with cauliflower, rocket and spinach, so soil moisture levels need to be constant.

BROWN ROT
A common fungus that attacks most tree fruits. Insect damage, bruising during harvesting and damage from apple scab are all responsible for allowing the disease entry. It is spread by spores carried on the wind, on insects or by physical contact between fruits.

SYMPTOMS: Brown patches and concentric rings of white fungus appear on fruit. May affect fruit on trees and in storage.

PREVENTION: Remove all damaged fruit and prune and dispose of dead branches and twigs and any mummified fruits that remain on the tree, as the disease can overwinter on these.

BUD DROP
Poor flowering or flower buds drop without opening. Runner beans are the main crop affected.

SYMPTOMS: Buds drop before pollination causing poor or no crop.

PREVENTION: Prepare soil well in order to retain moisture. Water regularly. Use companion plants that encourage pollinating insects.

CHLOROSIS
Raspberries and other acid-loving plants can suffer from lime-induced chlorosis.

SYMPTOMS: Yellowing of the leaves between the veins. Confirm diagnosis by testing the soil to see if it is alkaline.

PREVENTION AND TREATMENT: Work acidic manures and fertilisers into the soil. Mulch with acidic organic matter.

CHOCOLATE SPOT
Fungal disease of broad beans which is seldom serious.

SYMPTOMS: Dark brown spots on foilage and stems.

PREVENTION: The chocolate spot fungus overwinters in plant debris or soil, so be careful about garden hygiene and destroy infected material. Avoid overcrowding plants.

CLUB ROOT
This serious fungal infection affects cabbages and other brassicas, turnips, swedes and radishes.

SYMPTOMS: Thickening of the roots, which become distorted into a large swollen mass. A diseased plant is stunted, may have discoloured, and will have sickly foilage.

PREVENTION: Improve the soil texture and drainage by digging in compost or leafmould. Lime the soil. Use crop rotation because this is a soil-borne disease. Keep down cruciferous weeds such as charlock, wild radish and shepherd's purse as these can harbour the disease. Destroy infected plants.

Some gardeners believe that putting a few small pieces of rhubarb (leaves or stems) in the planting hole when transplanting brassica seedlings will control clubroot.

CROWN ROT
Bacterial disease of rhubarb.

SYMPTOMS: Discoloured leaves, followed by stalks and crown rotting.

PREVENTION: As condition is caused by wet soil conditions, improve drainage. Destroy infected plants and do not plant rhubarb in the same position again.

CUCUMBER MOSAIC VIRUS
Viral disease of cucumbers and other cucurbits. The virus overwinters in many perennial weed sources, and is especially attractive to aphids when weed growth resumes in the spring.

SYMPTOMS: Yellowish mottling of leaves and fruit. Plants growth is stunted and fruits puckered.

PREVENTION: Control aphids as they are the main cause of the spread of this virus. Control weeds such as common chickweed. Destroy infected plants.

DAMPING OFF

Fungal disease of seedlings.

SYMPTOMS: Stems rot at soil level causing the seedlings to topple over. Occurs particularly in crowded sowings in wet, cold soils and in unsterile composts, trays and pots.

PREVENTION: Good hygiene is important. Use only sterilised containers and fresh compost. Sow seeds thinly and prick out as soon as the true leaves begin to appear. It is probably better to use tap water rather than water from a butt. Avoid water-logging the growing medium (use a fine rose or spray mister to water gently).

DOWNY MILDEW

Attacks brassicas, lettuces, onions and spinach.

SYMPTOMS: Yellow blotches appear on the upper leaf surface with corresponding greyish-white fungal growth on the lower surface.

PREVENTION: Avoid damp conditions, space the plants well and maintain good weed control to ensure airflow through the crop. Remove all infected leaves and destroy promptly, to prevent spread of the disease and contamination of the soil by resting spores. Do not compost infected material. Ensure that related weed hosts are not present. Maintain as long a rotation as possible.

GREY MOULD

This very common fungal disease affects a wide range of plants including strawberries and raspberries.

SYMPTOMS: In humid conditions, affected plants will be covered in a fuzzy grey layer of fungus. When humidity is low, plant parts may still rot and shrivel, but without the grey fungus.

PREVENTION: On soft fruit little can be done to prevent infection other than prompt removal of infected material to limit disease spread. Dead plant material should be removed and destroyed. Hard surfaces should be regularly cleaned and sterilised. Air circulation should be maintained to avoid high humidity and reduce spore production.

NECK ROT

Rot occurring in stored onions.

SYMPTOMS: Grey velvety mould found on the neck of stored onions which go on to rot.

PREVENTION: Aim to produce hard, well-ripened bulbs. Avoid excessive nitrogen and any fertilisers which will produce soft growth. Should not be applied after July. Damaged or thick-neck bulbs should be removed immediately. Ensure the plants are dry before storing in a cool dry place.

POWDERY MILDEW

This name is used for a number of fungal diseases that affect a range of plants; producing similar symptoms.

SYMPTOMS: White powdery coating on leaves, shoots and flowers.

PREVENTION: Keep plants well watered and mulch to preserve soil moisture. Keep good air-flow around plants to reduce humidity by avoiding overcrowding. Keep crops clear of weeds. Avoid high nitrogen fertilisers, as these encourage soft sappy growth that is more susceptible to mildew.

TREATMENT: Some vegetable crops and fruits, including vines, can be treated with sulphur dust. Check instructions carefully as certain gooseberry and apple cultivars may be damaged by sulphur.

VIRUS DISEASES

A wide range of disorders enter plant tissues and produce varied symptoms on a variety of plants.

SYMPTOMS: Viruses are probably the hardest type of disease to diagnose. Typical symptoms include colour changes in leaves, stunted growth and wilting.

PREVENTION: Viruses can be spread by infected insects that carry the disease, including aphids, thrips, whiteflies and leafhoppers. They can also be spread by infected plants or contaminated hands or garden tools. Treat aphid and other insect infestations promptly. Practice good garden hygiene. Wash soil off tools after use. Thoroughly clean and disinfect tools and plant pots and seed trays at the end of the season. Wash your hands after handling diseased plant matter to avoid infecting healthy plants with vegetable diseases.

GLOSSARY

GLOSSARY

ACID RAIN — Rainwater that contains sulphur dioxide and other industrial pollutants.

ACID SOIL — Soil that is lower than 7.0 pH (higher would be alkaline). Acidity is measured by the amount of calcium in the soil, as is alkaline soil.

AERATION — The loosening of soil by digging or other mechanical means to allow air to pass freely, usually done on lawns.

AEROBIC — Usually used for describing a characteristic of compost heaps. Describes organisms living or occurring only in the presence of oxygen.

ALKALINE SOIL — Soil that has a pH level of more than 7.

ALLELOPATHY — The release of chemicals by certain plants that will prevent the growing of other plants in close proximity.

AMENDMENT — Usually referring to some form of organic material being added to the soil for the purpose of improvement.

ANAEROBIC — Describes organisms living or occurring when oxygen is absent. Usually refers to compost heaps.

ANNUAL — A plant that will complete its life cycle in one growing season.

APHIDS — Small sap-sucking insects. They infect foliage and are easily recognised by the sugary 'honey dew' that they secrete, often attracting ants.

ASEXUAL — This is a means of propagation that does not include seed production but by cuttage, dividing and layering.

BT — *Bacillus thuringiensis*. A bacterium which will destroy the stomach cells of insects that consume it. This biological insecticide will also kill young butterfly caterpillars.

BACKFILL — Replacing dirt from the original hole after planting.

BARE ROOT — Plants that have been dug out of the ground when dormant.

BEDDING PLANT — Usually an annual plant temporarily in a garden display.

BENEFICIAL INSECT — Insects that will improve and work in our gardens.

BIENNIAL — A plant that will require two growing seasons to complete its life cycle.

BIOLOGICAL PEST CONTROL — Using living organisms such as beneficial insects or parasites to destroy garden pests.

BLACK SPOT — A fungal disease on the foliage of roses, caused by moisture.

BLANCH — To keep light from the leaves and stems, keeping the plant tissue soft.

BLOSSOM END ROT — A cultural deficiency created by a lack of calcium. Most common in peppers and tomatoes.

BOLT — Annual vegetables or flowers that grow quickly to flowering stage, and go to seed before reaching their full potential.

BONEMEAL — A fertiliser made from crushed animal bones.

BOTANICAL NAME — The Latin scientific name of a plant is its botanical name.

BRACT — A modified leaf, sometimes coloured and can be mistaken for a petal: for example the Poinsettia and Bougainvillea.

BROADCAST — A method by which seeds or fertiliser are scattered randomly to cover an area.

BROWN ROT — A fungus frequently found on fruit.

BUD — The embryonic shoot on a stem, branch or tuber. It is the start of a flower.

BULB — A storage organ, usually formed below ground level, used for propagation.

BULBIL — An immature small bulb formed on the stem of a plant.

BUSH — A many branched small shrub with no distinct main stems.

CALLUS — Scar tissue that forms when a plant has been damaged or cut.

CAMBIUM — The thin membrane that grows just under the bark of a plant.

CANE — A slender, straight, not very woody branch or stem of a plant (i.e. bamboo).

CANKER — An area on soft or rotten woody stems or twigs that is caused by bacteria and fungi.

CHLOROPHYLL — The green pigment in leaves.

CLOCHE — A cover for protecting plants from the cold.

CLONE — A genetically identical group of plants created from one individual by vegetative propagation.

CLUB ROOT — A disease of cabbages and some related vegetables caused by the slime mould fungus.

COLD COMPOST — A method by which organic material just rots on its own.

COMMON NAME — The name by which plants are known by non-botanists.

COMPACTION — Created by heavy machinery squeezing the layers of the soil together. This means the soil is no longer of good texture for planting.

COMPANION PLANTING — Different plants that are planted together for the benefit of each other.

COMPLETE FERTILISER — A fertiliser that can provide all the three main elements: nitrogen, phosphorus and potassium.

COMPOST — A term for decomposed organic matter.

CONIFER — An evergreen, coniferous tree or shrub generally bearing cones.

CORDON — A fruit tree which is repeatedly pruned and trained to grow as a single rope-like stem.

CORM — A swollen, underground stem base used for propagation.

COTYLEDON — The first set of leaves to grow after a seed has germinated.

CROSS POLLINATION — The transfer of pollen from the flower of one plant to the flower on a different plant.

CROWN — The region where shoot and root join, usually at or very near the ground level.

CULINARY HERB — A plant grown for its strong flavour which is used in cooking.

CULTIVATE — Breaking the topsoil so water and air can penetrate, and, to prevent weeds.

CULTIVATION — The technique of working the soil.

CULTIVAR — Used when determining plant names. Indicates the variety originated in cultivation and not the wild.

CUT BACK — Trimming or cutting moderately, making sure some of the last season's growth is left, to clean the plant up and the encourage new growth.

CUTTING — A leaf, roots, shoot, stem or a bud that has been cut off and then used in propagation.

DAMPING OFF — A decayed young seedling at ground level, caused by a fungal attack.

DAPPLED SHADE — Partial shade that is created by allowing sun to shine through.

DARK-DEPENDENT SEEDS — Seeds that germinate only in darkness.

DAY LENGTH — This is the number of hours from sunrise to sunset.

DAY NEUTRAL — A plant whose blooming period is not affected by the length of day.

DEADHEADING — To remove dead flowerheads that have already bloomed.

DECIDUOUS — Plants that lose their leaves at the end of the growing season.

DETHATCH — The process of taking up dead grass and plant material that builds up under the grass making the soil easier to absorb nutrients.

DIBBER — A tool used to make holes for seeds or bulbs.

DIEBACK — A process caused by disease or pests, affecting the tips of branches and shoots.

DIOCECIOUS — A plant which bears either male of female flowers.

DIRECT SEEDING — Putting seeds directly in the soil as opposed to transplanting seedlings.

DISBUDDING — This refers to fruit crops and means to selectively take off buds to diminish the crop production to improve quality.

DISTILLED WATER — Pure water free from dissolved salts.

DIVISION — A method of propagating plants by separating each one into two or more sections and then repotting.

DORMANT PERIOD (DORMANCY) — The time when a plant has naturally stopped growing and the leaves have fallen, or the top growth has died down.

DOUBLE DIGGING — A method of deep cultivation.

DOUBLE FLOWER — A flower that is full from overlapping petals.

DOWNY MILDEW — A certain kind of mildew caused by a special fungi.

DRAINAGE — How water moves through the soil.

DRIP IRRIGATION — A trickle irrigation system. Highly recommended for soaking the soil well.

DWARF — Shorter than its normal growth.

EDGING PLANT — On the edge or border of a bed.

EFFLORESCENCE — The deposit of calcium and fertiliser salts on the outer surfaces of clay pots.

ENDEMIC — Plants which come from a certain geographical area.

EROSION — The wearing away of soil created by man, rain or wind.

ESPALIER — The method of training a tree or shrub to grow in a pattern.

EVAPOTRANSPIRATION — The amount of water that transpires through a plant's leaves combined with the amount that evaporates from the soil in which it is growing.

EVERGREEN — A plant that will bear foliage throughout the year.

EXOTIC — Plants that are native to other parts of the world and have been introduced here.

EYE — An undeveloped growth bud (as in a potato).

F1 — Breeders use this term and it refers to the first generation offspring from two plants that have been bred.

F2 — The product of two F1 plants that have been crossed.

FAIRY RING — A circle of fungal growth.

FASCIATION — A genetic mutation or imbalance in growth caused by absorption of a herbicide.

FAMILY — One genus or several genera which have a basically similar floral pattern make up a family (i.e. LILLACEAE — lily).

FERTILISE(RS) — The act of or the actual substance added to the soil to provide additional nutrients for plants.

FLORE PLENO — A botanical term describing a flower with extra petals.

FOLIAR FERTILISER — A liquid, water soluble, fertiliser applied to a plant's foliage in a fine spray.

FORCING — The process of making a plant grow or flower before its natural season.

FROND — A leaf of a fern or palm.

FROST — The freezing and condensation of moisture in the air.

FROST HARDY — Plants that are able to survive winter frosts without damage to their leaves.

FROST TENDER — These plants will be damaged or killed by even the lightest of winter frosts.

FRUIT FLY — A small insect pest that will lay its eggs beneath the surface of developing fruits.

FULL SHADE — This shade is sometimes called deep shade and is created by mature trees.

FULL SUN — Six hours or more in the direct sun during the growing season of the year.

FUNGICIDE — A chemical used to control diseases caused by fungi.

FUNGUS — A primitive form of plant life.

FUSARIUM — A fungal disease which is soil-borne and causes wilting and death mostly in herbaceous plants.

GALL — An unusual and abnormal growth on a plant.

GENUS — Used when naming plants. Genus is the plant equivalent of a surname.

GERMINATE — The sprouting of a seed.

GLASSHOUSE — Another name for a greenhouse.

GRAFTING — A method of propagation by joining a stem or bud of one plant (known as the scion) on to the stem of another (known as the stock).

GRANULAR FERTILISER — A fertiliser that is dry and in a tiny pellet form.

GREENHOUSE — A structure that can be build out of glass, plastic, or fibreglass in which the temperature is maintained within a desired range. Used for cultivating tender plants or growing plants out of season.

GREEN MANURE — A crop that is grown and then incorporated into the soil to increase soil fertility or organic matter content.

GROUND COVER — A plant used to provide a low-growing carpet between other plants.

GROWING HABIT — A direction or shape a plant takes as it grows.

GROWING POINT — The area where new growth appears.

HABIT — The shape or form of a plant.

HABITAT — The environment in which a plant is usually found growing.

HALF-HARDY — A plant that is not completely hardy.

HARDENING OFF — Gradual acclimatisation to colder conditions.

HARDINESS — When a plant has the ability to withstand low temperatures or frost.

HAY — Grass, clover, alfalfa, etc., cut and dried for use as forage. It is great for compost piles and using as a mulch.

HEART ROT — A plant disease in which the central part of a plant rots (especially in trees).

HEAVING — When there is a climate change from frost to warming of the soil, often causing the soil to buckle upwards.

HEDGE — A row of bushes or small trees planted close together to form a fence or boundary.

HEDGEROW — A row of bushes or trees forming a hedge.

HEEL CUTTING — A short, side branch taken as a cutting with a small piece of the main stem.

HEELING-IN — This is a temporary planting procedure until a plant can be put in its permanent place.

HERB — A plant grown for its medicinal or flavouring qualities.

HERBACEOUS — A plant with a non-woody stem.

HERBICIDE — Any chemical that will kill a plant.

HONEY DEW — The sweet and sticky syrup secreted by aphids and other sap-sucking insects.

HORTICULTURE — The art and science of gardening.

HOST — Any plant material that will support a parasite.

HOT HOUSE — Another term for a greenhouse.

HUMUS — The organic residue of decayed vegetables in the soil (i.e. leaf mould or compost.)

HYBRID — The offspring of two different varieties or species.

HYDROPONICS — A method of growing a plant in water containing dilute nutrients.

INDIGENOUS — Plant species that are native to that region.

INFERTILE — Soil that has no nutrients.

INFLORESCENCE — A group or cluster of flowers arranged on a stem, or the flowerhead.

INORGANIC — A chemical or fertiliser which has been made using neither organic life nor the products of organic life.

INSECTICIDE — A synthetic or organic chemical used to kill or repel insects.

INSECTICIDAL SOAP — An alternative to using chemicals on plants — aka Soft Soap.

INSECTIVOROUS PLANT — Another term for carnivorous plants.

IN SITU — The act of sowing seeds or cuttings in the ground where they are to grow.

INTERCROPPING or INTERPLANTING — Mixing two or more plants, tall and short, for foliage difference, or combining plants that bloom at different times of the year.

INVASIVE — The ability of a plant to spread quickly and to crowd out other plantings.

KERNEL — The edible part of a nut.

LACEWING — A beneficial insect which will eat mites, aphids and thrip.

LANDSCAPE FABRIC — A method of smothering weeds, which can be a variety of materials, for example newspaper or black plastic.

LAYERING — The process of rooting branches, twigs or

stems that are still attached to a parent plant, as by placing a specially treated part in moist soil.

LEACHING — A process which can rid soils of bad substances, like salts.

LEADER — The main growing shoot of a sapling.

LEAF CUTTING — A method of propagation using the leaves of a plant.

LEAF MOULD — Partially decayed leaves.

LEAFLET — A leaf-like section of a compound leaf.

LEGGY — Tall and spindly growth, not usual to the growth habit of the plant, caused by lack of light.

LEGUME — The pod of a plant of the pea or bean family.

LICHEN — A combined growing condition of algae and fungus.

LITHOPHYTE — Plants that grow on rocks or other areas that do not need soil.

LOAM — Good quality soil in which adequate supplies of clay, sand and fiber are present.

MANURE — Any animal droppings with a high content of nitrogen. These need to be composted and aged before use.

MANURE TEA — A liquid fertiliser made by mixing manures with water and filtering out.

MARGINAL PLANT — Plants that will grow on the edges of ponds or lakes.

MASS PLANTING — The planting of one particular flower or many of the same kind in close proximity to create a dramatic effect.

MICROCLIMATE — A physical area with a set of conditions different from those surrounding the area.

MICRONUTRIENTS — Very important nutrients that plants need for proper growth.

MICRO-ORGANISMS — Animals and plants that are too small to be seen clearly with the naked eye but are the soil improvers.

MICRO-PROPAGATION — The practice of rapidly multiplying stock plant material to produce a large number of progeny plants.

MILDEW — Several different types of fungi.

MIST PROPAGATION — The ideal method of propagation in a greenhouse using automatic misters.

MIXED BORDER — A flower bed with a mix of different plants.

MONOECIOUS — A plant which bears both male and female flowers.

MOWING STRIP — Sometimes known as an edging strip. A space between the lawn and the flower or vegetable bed, often in cement or brick.

MULCH — Any loose, usually organic, material over the soil as a protective covering.

MUTATION — Any change in a plant which will lead to a new feature.

NATIVE — A plant that grows in the same habitat in which they originated.

NATURALISED — Plants that will behave like native plants in a given geological region.

NECTAR — A sugar and water substance secreted by flowers which attracts pollinators such as bees.

NEEM — A botanical insecticide that is non-toxic.

NEMATODE — A microscopic roundworm that lives in the soil.

NEUTRAL — This is neither acid nor alkaline: pH 6.5—7.5.

NEW WOOD — The part of a stem or branch that has grown during the current season.

NODE — The point on a stem where a leaf or bud is attached.

NODE ANCHORING — Node anchoring or node cuttings are when you take a cutting of a stem right below a node.

OFFSET — A young plantlet which appears on a mature plant.

OPEN POLLINATED — Any plant that has been pollinated in the meadow.

ORGANIC — Fertilisers and chemicals that have been obtained from a source which is or has been alive.

ORNAMENTAL — A plant that is grown strictly for its foliage or flower rather than for food.

OVER POTTING — Repotting a plant into a pot which is too large to allow successful establishment.

OVERSEEDING — Planting on top of an existing garden or lawn.

PALMATE LEAF — A leaf with five or more lobes arising from one point.

PARASITE — Any plant that grows upon another — mistletoe is a good example of a parasite.

PEAT — The preserved and compressed remains of dead bog plants.

PEAT POT — Compressed peat into a pot that can be used for starting seeds.

PEBBLE TRAY — A tray filled with pebbles to create humidity in the environment.

PERENNIAL — A plant which will live for three years or more under normal conditions.

PERFOLIATE — Paired leaves which fuse around the stem.

PERGOLA — Sometimes called an arbour, or walkway covered with trellis work.

PERLITE — Granular volcanic rock used to improve the aeration in potting soil.

PETAL — One of the divisions of the corolla.

pH — The scale where the acidity and alkalinity of soil is measured.

PHOTOPERIODISM — The response of plants to the length of a day and night.

PINCH OUT — Pinching with the fingers to remove the tip of a growing shoot to encourage lateral growth.

PLANTLET — A small plant off the original plant.

PLANT LICE — Otherwise known as aphids, these are small or even very small insects.

PLEACHING — A popular technique of training and pruning shrubs and trees into a wall.

PLUG — A small but well-rooted seedling raised in a cellular tray for covering large areas like ground covers or lawns.

POLLEN — The yellow dust produced to transport the male gamete (male DNA) to the female part of a flower.

POLLINATOR — The biotic agent that moves pollen from the male anthers of a flower to the female stigma to accomplish fertilisation.

POTAGER — A vegetable garden that is planted in a formal and ornamental style.

POT BOUND — A plant growing in a pot which is too small to allow proper leaf and stem growth.

POTPOURRI — A mixture of sweet smelling leaves, petals and blooms to create a perfume in a room.

POTTING UP — Taking the young seedlings or transplants into a larger container for mature growth.

PROPAGATION — The production of more plants by seeds, cuttings, grafting or other methods.

PRUNING — The cutting of leaves or branches within limits in order to remove dead or diseased foliage or branches.

RADICUMS — These plants are special in that their stems have roots that will cling as they grow vertically or grow over the ground: such as ivy.

RAISED BED — Any ornamental or vegetable bed that has soil higher than the surrounding immediate area.

REED — Tall grasses that grow in shallow water.

REMONTANT — Plants that will bloom more than once a year.

RE-SEEDING — Plants that drop their seeds for next season.

RESTING PERIOD — It is a period of dormancy where energy is restored to the plant.

RETAINING WALL — A wall that has been built on a slope to keep the soil from sliding or eroding.

REVERT — Sometimes a particular cultivar might change back to one of its original species.

RHIZOME — A thickened stem which grows horizontally below or on the soil surface: such as iris.

ROCK GARDEN — An area constructed of larger rocks arranged to look natural, and interspersed with plants.

ROOT BALL — Matted roots and the soil that is attached to them that you see when lifting a plant from a container or the ground.

ROOT-BOUND — Usually, when plants are left too long in their container the roots become entangled and begin to grow in circles.

ROOT CROPS — Any vegetable that the roots are edible: for example, carrots, potatoes and turnips.

ROOT CUTTING — Where the root is used for propagation.

ROOTING HORMONE — A chemical in powder or liquid form which promotes the formation of roots at the base of a cutting.

ROOT PRUNING — The practice of removing a portion of a tree's root system to promote further growth.

ROOT ROT — Common in plants that are affected by fungus diseases and have poor drainage.

ROOTSTOCK — The roots and stems arise from this part of the plant.

ROOT ZONE — The entire area where roots are growing below the plant.

ROTATION — The successive planting of different crops on the same land to improve soil fertility.

ROTENONE — Material, used a lot by organic gardeners, which is derived from the roots of tropical legumes.

RUN — A plant that runs will be growing rapidly underground. Great for ground cover.

RUNNER — A creeping stem which produces small plantlets along its length.

SAP — Fluid found in plants.

SAPLING — A very young tree.

SCALD — Discolouration which occurs when plants have been overexposed to sunlight.

SCALE — Sucking insects.

SCAPE — A leafless flower stem that will grow directly from the base of the stem.

SCARIFY — To scratch or break the hard coat of some seeds so they will germinate easily.

SCIENTIFIC NAME — The internationally recognised Latin name of a plant.

SCION — A specimen of a woody plant used in grafting.

SEEDHEAD — Dried, inedible fruit that contains seeds.

SELF POLLINATION — The transfer of pollen from one flower to another flower on the same plant.

SELF-SEEDED — A plant's habit of shedding seeds in the immediate area which then germinate without help.

SEMI-EVERGREEN — Shrubs that will keep some of their green foliage — typically in mild climates.

SET — Refers to shallot bulbs and small onions, as in sets of onions.

SHARP SAND — A rough sand to help with drainage and propagation.

SHEET COMPOSTING — A method of piling undecomposed organic materials over the soil and waiting for decomposition.

SHRUB — A woody plant with a framework of branches and little or no central stem.

SIDE DRESS — Placing fertiliser on the side of the plant material to encourage growth during the season.

SIEVE — A frame with a mesh bottom used to break down soil or compost.

SLOW RELEASE FERTILISER — A natural fertiliser that over a period of time will release its nutrients.

SOAKER HOSE — Hoses that have hundreds of mini holes to let the water out slowly and can be left on for a long period of time.

SOLARISATION — The process by which the soil is sterilised by the sun.

SOLUBLE FERTILISER — A fertiliser that is mixed with water.

SOOTY MILDEW — A small black fungus which grows on the honeydew produced by aphids and other insects.

SPECIES — A group of plants that have common characteristics.

SPENT — Bulbs and flowers of a plant that have finished blooming.

SPHAGNUM MOSS — Many mosses native to bogs are sphagnum. Often used for the lining of hanging baskets.

SPICES — Seeds, fruits, or roots (rhizomes) used to flavour cooking.

SPORE — A microscopic reproductive cell of non-flowering plants (i.e. ferns and mosses).

STANDARD — Those plants, especially roses, that are grown so all the branches are brought to a head on one single stem.

STEM CUTTING — A portion of a stem that only includes one or more nodes taken from a plant, used for propagation.

STERILISED SOIL — It is soil that is steam- or chemically-sterilised. Harmful organisms have been killed but helpful bacteria have been spared.

STIGMA — This is the part of the female organ of the flower which receives the pollen.

STOCK — The 'mother plant' of which cuttings are taken.

STONE — The inner fruit wall of a drupe (i.e. plums and cherries).

SUCCESSION PLANTING — Planting a fast crop one week or so after another with the object of keeping a constant supply on hand.

SUCCULENT — Succulent plants have leaves and/or stems which are thick and fleshy.

SUCKER — A shoot which arises from an underground shoot or root of a plant.

SUN SCORCH — Spots on leaves that are caused by exposure to strong sunlight.

STAKING — A means of support for tall plants.

SYSTEMIC INSECTICIDE — A pesticide which can be granular or liquid, used at the base of the plant and travels through the vascular stream.

TAMPING — Pressing the soil around a plant that has just been planted to make the sure soil is secure and firm around the roots.

TAP ROOT — The main root, sometimes swollen, which grows vertically into the soil.

TENDER — An indoor plant which requires a minimum temperature of 15°C (60°F).

TENDRIL — Plants producing a cordlike structure (like sweet peas, clematis and grapes) that will help to support themselves.

TERRESTRIAL — A plant which grows in the soil as opposed to aquatic or perched on trees.

THATCH — Any material that does not quickly decompose.

THICKET — Any area that has a lot of miscellaneous undergrowth.

THINNING — Picking out the overpopulated seedlings in any flower or vegetable bed.

THRIPS — Insects that feed on all parts of the plant.

TILL — Another definition for cultivating.

TIP CUTTING — A cutting taken from the top end of a shoot.

TIRED SOIL — A term referring to a piece of land that has been exhausted of its nutrient value.

TISSUE CULTURE — A sterile practice of propagating plants from the mother plant.

TOPIARY — The horticultural art of clipping and training woody plants to form geometric shapes or interesting patterns.

TOPDRESS — A process that means to apply on the surface of soil.

TOPSOIL — Soil that is on the very top, which contains a lot of humus and good elements needed for growth.

TRAILING — Any plant that grows long stems and will grow along the ground, rooting as it goes.

TRANSPIRATION — The loss of water through the pores of the leaf.

TRUG — A shallow basket for light chores, such as carrying flowers and fruits and vegtables.

TUBER — A storage organ used for propagation.

UNDERPLANTING — Growing short plants such as a ground cover under taller plants.

UNDER GLASS — A term referring to 'growing under glass'— essentially growing in a greenhouse.

VARIEGATED LEAF — A green leaf design which is blotched, edged, or spotted with yellow, white, or cream colour.

VERMICULITE — A lightweight mineral called mica that is added to potting mixtures to improve root growth.

VERTICILLIUM — A fungus disease that will cause wilting and death of a plant.

VIABILITY — The possibility of germination.

WEED — An unwanted plant in your garden.

WET FEET — A condition when the roots of plants are in standing water.

WHIP — A very thin shoot with no lateral branches of a woody plant.

WIDE ROW GARDENING — A method in which vegetables and cutting gardens are laid out usually two to three feet wide instead of a single file row of plants.

WILDFLOWER — Plants that can be native or exotic when growing out in a non-cultivated area.

WILT — A plant disease caused by bacteria or fungi.

WIND BREAK — Hedges and trees planted to act as shelter.

WINTER KILL — A condition that happens when plants have not hardened enough to withstand severe winter conditions.

WOODY PLANT — These are usually perennial plants that have permanent stems.

WORM (*eisenia foetida*) — Mother Nature's natural composter.